Humanism *and* Nationalism *in* TAGORE'S NOVELS

KH. KUNJO SINGH

ATLANTIC
PUBLISHERS & DISTRIBUTORS

Published by
ATLANTIC PUBLISHERS AND DISTRIBUTORS
B-2, Vishal Enclave, Opp. Rajouri Garden, New Delhi-27
Phones : 5413460, 5429987, 5466842

Sales Office
4215/1, Ansari Road, Darya Ganj, New Delhi-02
Phones : 3273880, 3285873, 3280451
Fax : 91-11-3285873
web : www.atlanticbooks.com
e-mail : info@atlanticbooks.com

ISBN 81-269-0184-5

Typeset at
APD Computer Graphics, Delhi
Printed in India at
Nice Printing Press, Delhi

DEDICATED TO

My loving mother
Late Smt. Kh. Tombi Devi
Under whose inspiring guidance
I learnt the first lessons
of the alphabet....

Preface

The corpus of the works of Rabindranath Tagore, the first Nobel laureate for literature in Asia, have been a popular field of study for more than half a century. Extensive critical enquiry has been made into his poetic creations. In spite of his being an outstanding Indo-Anglian poet, prophet, philosopher, novelist and essayist, much critical attention has not been accorded on his fictional creations. Some research has been conducted in recent years but these studies too, do not deal with all the major aspects, especially humanism and nationalism, available in all Rabindranath Tagore's novels in English translations. Hence, the need for this study.

Humanism and Nationalism in Tagore's Novels is purely a product of my original research in the field and it is designed as a reference book for post-graduate and M.Phil. students, and Ph.D. researchers of the universities in India and abroad.

I shall feel rewarded if this book succeeds in winning the attention of the scholars for the study of Tagore literature. A *Select Bibliography* has been given in the end both by way of acknowledgment and by way of bringing to the notice of scholars the materials available in the field.

While presenting this book to our enlightened readers, it is my sincere hope that it will be considered a worthwhile addition to the critical writings on Rabindranath Tagore.

I take this opportunity to thank and put on record the help provided by the library staff at Nombol L. Sanoi College, Nambol; Manipur University, Canchipur; Visva-Bharati University, Santiniketan; M/s Subarnarekha Book Stall, Visva-Bharati University, Campus; Gauhati University, Guwahati; National

Library, Calcutta; Sahitya Akademi, New Delhi and Rabindra Bharati University, Calcutta.

I am deeply indebted to Prof. Subhas Chandra Saha, Vice-Chancellor, Assam University, Sichar, Assam for inspiring me in the choice of this subject.

I sincerely thank my loving sons—Kh. Gourachandra Singh, Kh. Dhiren Singh, Kh. Devananda Singh and Kh. Premjit Singh who constantly helped me in the collection of materials for this study and accompanied me on many of my journeys to different libraries throughout the country.

I continue to be indebted to Shri A. Tejamani Singh and Y. Indrajit Singh both of whom happened to be Ph.D. research scholars under my supervision for helping me in different ways towards the completion of this work.

I am also deeply beholden to my octogenarian father, Shri Kh. Chandrahas Singh for his constant and ungrudging help during the course of this work. My heartfelt thanks also go to my loving wife, Mrs. Memcha Devi who silently put up with every inconvenience caused by my academic preoccupation.

Last but not the least, my thanks are also due to M/s Atlantic Publishers & Distributors, B-2, Vishal Enclave, Opposite Rajouri Garden, New Delhi-27, India for undertaking the publication of this book successfully within a short time.

1st August, 2002 **KH. KUNJO SINGH**

CONTENTS

1

Introducing Rabindranath Tagore

To introduce Rabindranath Tagore is like to introduce an age. He is really a phenomenon. His unique merit lies in his quantity, his immense range and his fabulous variety. He is our Chaucer and Shakespear, our Dryden and our equivalent of the English translators of the Bible. He compresses in one man's (his) lifetime the development of several centuries. He has created language, both prose and verse. The range of his verse technique carries us from Wyatt and Surrey, across Spenser, Marlowe, Dryden, Shelley and Swinburne, right upto the early Ezra Pound. His narrative verse, verse dramas and lyrics are momentous works. His ballads excel Scott's; his child poems blend Blake's innocence with an almost sophisticated humour of Chaucer. He has introduced psychological novel and marvellous short stories. His criticism is profuse and fundamental, his satire occasional and brilliant. His travel diaries are rich in both observation and contemplation. He has created a new form of the prose-play and has written on philosophy, education, politics, science, prosody, music and peasantry. He has done all, all that can be done with written word. So Buddhadeva Bose remarks: "Rabindranath is the world's most complete writer."[1]

The Indian Renaissance began with Raja Rammohan Roy. There was not a department of life—religion, social reform, education, journalism, public administration, legislation—which did not receive the beneficial impact of his personality and he is described as "the first of our latter-day Mahapurushas."[2]

Rammohan's work was continued by the Tagores who were affluent, distinguished, in many ways exclusive, if not alienated. Rabindranath's grandfather, Dwarkanath, who built the family fortune was known as a "prince" and his father, "Maharshi" Devendranath was an austerer personality. His *Autobiography* is compared with the *Testament* of Ignatius Loyola, the *Journal* of George Fox. He abandoned the orthodox Hindu ways and became the leader of Brahmo Samaj (Brahmo brotherhood).

Rabindranath was born on Tuesday May 7, 1861, in the ancestral mansion, Jorasanko (at present known as Maharshi Bhavan) at 6 Dwarkanath Tagore Lane , in central Calcutta as the youngest of the eight sons (and the fourteenth child) of Maharshi Debendranath (44). His mother Sarada Devi (37) could not provide caress to him as she was busy in looking after a huge, sprawling family. He spent his early days under the reign of servocracy. He led a rather Spartan life. Apart from tutors, there was a wrestling master too. In due course he was sent to several schools. But the formal education did not suit him and finally he became a dropout. The confined life at home whetted his sensibility, the hunger of the eye and the mind. Joy and mystery became two of the major motives of his creative life. He found them from the world of man and Nature around him.

The dual influence of the Maharshi and the Himalayas schooled the boy in thoughts, elemental and sublime, while the Gayatri mantra proved and perennial source of strength and joy. Though he had no regular schooling he had a profound regard for some of the Jesuit Fathers of St. Xavier's College, Calcutta. His forerunners in literature—Madhusudan, Iswar Chandra Vidyasagar, and Bankim Chandra influenced him to start with Bengali poetry, prose and fiction and it was an atmosphere of expectancy. He eagerly breathed this air of infinite possibility. Moreover, music and piety were part of the Tagore household. He wrote teenager plays and poems. The following is the sample of the juvenilia:

Come, my maiden gay, my heartless beauty.
What did I tell them over and over again?
The wound has split the bottom of my heart.
My mind and heart, O how they burn![3]

At a very young age he was powerfully drawn to the Vaishnava Singers and their lyrics (Padavalis), and he wrote a youthful imitation, *Bhanusinger Padavali* ("Bhanu" means the sun, that is Robi.), thus:

The bower is covered with flowers,
It echoes with the sound of the flute.
Casting off fear and shame,
Come, O dear one, come.[4]

A visit to England followed, and the English romantics—Byron, Shelley, Keats, Wordsworth—and the great Victorians, Tennyson and Browning, exercised a potent influence on Tagore. He also admired Shakespeare, Milton, Sir Thomas Browne, and Pope. He also wrote serious essays on Anglo-Saxon poetry, Dante, Goethe and Petrarch. The year and a half at the London University were pleasant but abortive. He never completed the course possibly to join the Bar or the Civil Service. So his father called him back. Prior to his stay in England, he spent sometime at Ahmedabad, with his civilian brother, Satyendranath. The house where he stayed provided the background for his fantasy, "Hungry Stones." Also here he became familiar with an attractive emancipated Maharashtrian girl, Anna Tarkhas (Anna Turkhar or Ana Turkhud).

Bhagna Hridaya (Broken Heart) shows the lingering of memory. Tagore's own words are explicit: "I have never been able to forget her."[5] This romantic agony can be felt in *Sandhya Sangeet* (Evening Songs). The way out was less through the Bankimesque novel, *Bau Thakuranir Hat* (The Young Queen's Mart) than through the euphoric *Prabhat Sangeet* (Morning Song). Another exposure of the interior milieu was in the play *Prakritir Pratishodh* (Nature's Revenge). To Tagore the contrast between the life of normal emotion and ascetic rejection is basic. When the ascetic returns to the outcaste, abandoned girl, she is dead. Nature has taken her revenge. The ascetic draws the moral: "The Great is to be found in the small, the Infinite in bounded forms." The experience would run through all his life. Besides, he had written about 7000 lines of verse before he was 18, and this pace he maintained for the greater part of his life.

Back in Calcutta, Rabindranath married on December 9, 1883, a plain girl, Mrinalini Devi—the daughter of one of the junior officers of the family estate. Within six months of the marriage his pet sister-in-law, Kadambari Devi, wife of Jyotirindranath, committed suicide. The mystery has never been solved. Years later he was to offer a remarkable tribute to her in "Chhabi" (picture); "the poet in the heart of a poet."[6]

For some time he worked as the Secretary of the Brahmo Samaj taking up cudgels against the proponents of neo-Hinduism and would not spare even Bankimchandra. On the request from a Calcutta-based Ladies Club (Sakhi Samaj) he wrote a play for an all women cast. It was *Mayar Khela* (The Play of Illusion). Its refined and erotic verse, *bhalo bese jadi sukha nahi* (if there is no joy in love) became a popular hit song. The novel *Rajarshi* (The Royal Sage), later adapted as a verse-play *Visarjan* (Sacrifice) was a moving indictment of the Hindu ritual of offering human sacrifice.

Rabindranath was also an effective and efficient landlord. But he was also the lord of poetry, of realms of gold. At Shelaidah on a sultry day appeared the magical line: *gagane garaje megh ghanavarasha* (the heavy rainclouds clap in the sky). This was worked out into one of his finest poems, *Sonar Tari* (Golden Boat). Many of the *Sonar Tari* poems were written in peripatetic fashion. He has seen as well as made his life a *Chirajatra*, an endless journey.

By this time Rabindranath spoke publicity on "The vicissitudes of Education" (*Sikshar Herpher*) where he emphasised on the use of mother tongue. He also spoke on political situation. Another venture, literary but non-paying, the journal *Sadhana* had to be wound up. Idleness in a rural retreat helped him to mix with the common people and he brought out his excellent short stories, *Galpaguchha* (Bunch of stories).

It was about this time that Rabindranath wrote *Malini, Chaitali* and Baikunther Khata (Vaikantha's Manuscript). These were followed by *Panchbhuter Diary* (The Diary of the Five Elements), a dialogue, a delightful comedy, *Chirkumar Sabha* and the somewhat pagan *Chaitali* poems. In 1901, Rabindranath wrote *Naivedya* containing the remarkable line: "Deliverance is not for me in renunciation."[7]

Rabindranath played a new role when he started a school for children at Santiniketan (December 21, 1901). The students, five in all, were dressed in ochre robes. And he himself remarked: "The growth of the school is the growth of my life."[8] Shortly after, his self-effacing wife, who shared his work, died. A widower at forty-one, he spoke of his "broken abode" in *Smaran* (Remembrance). A little after his little daughter, Rani also passed away. But he continued writing and added some poems to the volume of children's verse, *Sishu* (Crescent Moon). He also contributed seriously to the prestigious journal, *Bangadarshan.* Tagore had a strong faith in young idealists. But the death of Satis Chandra Ray, one of the brightest teachers, was a great blow to him. Some other talented teachers also left the school. So for a time the school had to be shifted elsewhere.

As a result of the British game of divide-and-rule, the partition of Bengal (*Bangabhanga*) was in the offing. This policy of Lord Curzon was strongly resented. Tagore was deeply involved. In his essay on *Swadeshi Samaj* he analysed the grass-root problem of a truly Indian social policy. He expressed nationalist enthusiasm eloquently in his poem on Shivaji (August 1904). The date of partition (October 16, 1905) drew near and the attitude of the people stiffened. Boycott of British goods was announced. In Calcutta's Town Hall Tagore read a paper, "The Situation and the Remedy" (*Abastha O Byabastha*) recommending the setting up of a parallel government. Everybody sang his songs. Young martyrs went up the gallows singing snatches of a Tagore song. He also wrote, "Sonar Bangla" (Golden Bengal), the national anthem of Bangla Desh. Tagore took part in a procession singing his own song—"Let the hearts of our people be one."

The idea of boycott included an alternative education through National Schools (Jatiya Vidyalaya). Everywhere there were protest meetings. When the fiery idealist, Aurobindo, the then Principal of the National College, was charged with sedition, Rabindranath wrote a deeply felt verse tribute—"Aurobindo, accept Rabindra's Namaskar." Indeed, Tagore was averse to violence and politics of assassination. Seeking for an alternative he began the work of rural reconstruction in his country estate at Sriniketan. He suffered the "Crowning tragedy" of his life at the death of his pet boy, Shamindra in November, 1907. He also became deeply aware of Indian Culture. His poem "Indian Pilgrimage" shows his cultural synthesis. We can quote the following remarkable line, "From the shore of vast humanity none will turn back or be turned back."[9]

Now Tagore began to look beyond the international horizon and the urgencies of politics. In the play *Prayaschitta* (Atonement) he presented a singing Baul—like Sashu, Dhananjay, with his message of love. He was perhaps anticipating Gandhi. The idea of the universal Man (*Visvamanav*) was slowly taking shape in his mind. Elsewhere he spoke of *Tapovan* (forest hermitage) and *Visvabodh* (world-awareness). He was writing *Gitanjali*, the winner of the covetous Nobel Prize.

Rabindranath's fiftieth birthday was celebrated at Santiniketan. The same year his incomplete autobiography *Jivansmriti* (reminiscences) was published. It was followed by *Raja* (The King of the Dark Chamber). His religious ideas were changing. His satire on a hidebound society in *Achalayatan* (The Immovables Edifice) was strongly resented by the orthodox. "*Janaganamana*" which was to become the Indian national anthem was written for the Congress session in Calcutta in 1911.

A little later on account of sudden illness his trip to England had to be cancelled. To recoup he went to Shilaidah. This is where the English version of *Gitanjali* took shape. Ultimately on May 27, 1912 he sailed for England. In England he handed over the manuscript of Gitanjali to William Rothenstein. All who met or heard him were overwhelmed. W.B. Yeats was the most enthusiastic of all. India Society and later Macmillan, published the book.

The poet went to America to lecturer on Religion, Culture and Race relations leaving the book to its fate. Very soon Gitanjali was gaining ground. There came favourable responses from many critics. Even Yeats had carried the manuscript with him "for days, reading it in railway trains, on the top of omnibuses, and in restaurants." Andrew Bradley remarked: "It looks as though we have at last a great poet among us."[10] After he had returned to India, the news of the award of the Nobel Prize for Literature on his Gitanjali came to Rabindranath on November 19, 1913. The award carried a sum of £ 8,000. Tagore's only comment on it was: "Henceforth I shall have no peace."[11]

Tagore's mood changes from the soft, sad songs of *Gitimalya and Gitali* to a rushing, restless temper in *Balaka* (Flight of Swans, 1916). He contributed to the avant garde journal *Sabuj Patra* (Green Leaves) striking a youthful note, passionate, protestant. His concern with the lot of women, as revealed in Strir Patra (The Wife's Letter), *Nasta Need* and *Ghare Baire* (The Home and the World) annoyed the orthodox. He also wrote *Phalguni* (The Cycle of Spring) in which he appeared in a dual role, that of the poet and the Baul, or wandering minstrel.

Tagore met Mahatma Gandhi on March 6, 1915 at Santiniketan. This was the beginning of a long friendship. Next year he was to visit America via Japan. In Japan, in the beginning, he was lavishly feted. But as soon as he started to speak against the evil of Nationalism, the welcome changed to indifference. Finally, this American lecturer programme had to be cancelled.

But this fruitless journey enabled Tagore to produce two books, *Personality* and *Nationalism*.

In spite of his open criticism of Nationalism Tagore was not anti-national. He protested against the repressive measures of the British India Government. Then came the Jalianwala Bagh Massacre on April 13, 1919 when the police fired on an unarmed crowd at Amritsar and killed many. The press was gagged. When the news leaked out, Tagore strongly protested and returned his Knighthood. During this time his play, *Dakghar* (Post Office) was produced in the Jorasanko Mansion before an audience decorated with Annie Besant, Mohondas Karamchand Gandhi and Madan Mohan Malviya. Then Tagore wrote *Lipika*, a prelude to the later prose poems.

In 1920 Tagore visited England again. This time the British were cold towards him because of his rejection of the then Knighthood. Then he went over to Paris, where he met Bergson, Sylvain Levy and others, including Comtesse de Noalis. Crowded Lecture tours of the Netherlands followed. But when he reached America there was studied indifference everywhere. Later, there were some programmes in Texas. There he gained a friend in the young Englishman, L.K. Elmhirst, who was to become a source of strength in his rural experiment in Sriniketan. "Things improved when, on the way back, he visited Switzerland. He had a splendid welcome in Germany. His sixtieth birthday was celebrated with fanfare. In Copenhagen, he was greeted with a torchlight procession. In Upsala he was requested to speak from the church altar, an unheard honour. In Darmstadt he spent about a week in Count Keyserling's Wisdom School. It was known as the Tagore Week."[12]

The poet returned to India in July 1921. Things in India were not happy. Gandhiji had started Non-Co-operation Movement. Political discussions took much of Tagore's time. On the creative side he wrote *Saradotsav* (Autumn Festival), a perennial school favourite. On December 21, 1921 Visva-Bharati was dedicated as a public trust with Elmhirst as the overall Director. The work of

Rural Reconstruction got a fillip as money had come from America.

His mind was on the other things as well. *Raktakarabi* (Red Oleanders) showed his grasp of the increasing dehumanisation of life in an industrial society based on a manipulation of resources, human and non-human. He was on the side of Life and Nature. By the same time he accepted an invitation to visit China. This enabled him to open a close cultural contact between the two countries. Soon after on the eve of his visit to Peru sudden illness came to him and he was advised complete rest. But a charming hostess, Victoria Ocampo, at her country estate in San Isidro, offered him hospitality. Between the two there sprang up an intimacy. The volume *Purabi*, containing delicate love poems, was dedicated to her.

Mahatma Gandhi visited Santiniketan in May, 1925. Tagore and Gandhi discussed many national issues, including Charkha, the theory and practice of spinning wheel. Two of Tagore's essays, on "Charkha" and "Swaraj", have stood the test of time. A little later two Italian scholars came to Santiniketan bearing gifts from Signor Mussolini. Tagore was delighted to see his institution internationalised and he sent a telegram thanking II Duce. Towards the end of the year he delivered the Presidential Address at the first All India Philosophy Congress held in Calcutta. He spoke more on the poetry of the Bauls whom he like most. Thenceforth he had even been called "Robi Baul."

He made a short but pleasant visit to Dacca and East Bengal. It revived his memories. This happiness was short-lived. On return to Calcutta he found poor, helpless victims in his Jorasanko Mansion. They were seeking refuge to avoid a communal riot. By the same time retouching a Buddhist theme, he produced *Natir Puja* (The Worship of the Dancing Girl), the moving story of a martyrdom. Tagore was a pace-setter in bringing out girls from educated families on the public stage.

Soon after he made a state visit to Italy. The party was lavishly feted. Tagore gave out his favourable impression about

Italy under Mussolini. Later on when he met Romain Rolland, he saw many of his encomiums over a Fascist regime. Tagore wrote a disclaimer to *The Manchester Guardian*, pleading innocence, wise after the event. From Italy he moved to England, Norway, Germany and Central Europe. By the side of Lake Balaton, where he took rests, stands an inscription of "the poet who loves while he lived."[13] He had planted a sapling that still lives. From there he went to Belgrade, Sofia, Bucharest, Istanbul, Athens and Cairo. When he returned to India (December 1926), Communal riots loomed large. Swami Shraddhananda who had visited Santiniketan, was killed by a fanatic.

Tagore wanted to renew India's lost cultural contact with the Far East. So he would be on the high seas again. Financed by the Birlas, Tagore, with a party of six, visited Singapore, Malaya, Java, Borneo, Sumatra and Indonesia. He was touched by the friendliness of welcome. The poem *Sagarika* (Sea Maiden) is a fine tribute and thanksgiving. He had planned a three-generation novel *Yogayog* which was never completed. But the completed part is an impressive record of the conflict between male chauvinism and sensitive womanhood.

Shortly after he went to Canada on the invitation by the National Council of Education. There he spoke on "The philosophy of Leisure." Back home, he was interested in introducing Japanese art of self-defence among his girl students. He delivered the Hibbert Lecture at Oxford in 1930. His theme was "The Religion of Man" which turned out to be the religion of an artist and a poet's confession of faith. In the meantime he took up painting hobby and participated in an art exhibition at Paris. He received fine appreciation.

A little later there was an exhibition in Berlin. He had a memorable but inconclusive conversation with Einstein. Tagore was taken to *Oberammargau* to see the Passion Play. His only poem in English, "The child" was clearly born of this visit. It is an unusual, impressive work with a mixture of myths and motives. The vision of history, with which the poem opens, is something new in Tagore. The martyrdom would seem to presage the killing of the Mahatma: "In his death the great victim lives in the life of all of us."[14]

He visited Moscow on the invitation of Russian government with a small party. He called it "Pilgrimage." It was in many ways a novel experience. He was most impressed by the progress of education and co-operatives. After it he visited New York where his paintings were exhibited. Shortly after it, he returned to India. His seventieth birthday was held throughout the country. Speaking at the mango grove, at Santiniketan, he underlined his self-image in a simple phrase: "*Ami Kavi,*" I am a poet, by nature a believer in totality."[15]

By this time the Indian national scene looked bleak as the Second Round Table Conference in London ended in smoke. In India the Gandhi-Willingdon Pact had been virtually dishonoured. Soon after Tagore arrived India the Mahatma was arrested. Tagore protested the government policy. Meanwhile, Reza Shah Pehlavi of Iran invited him to Iran. His seventieth birthday was celebrated in Tehran. A garland of seventy roses greeted the happy poet. From there he went to Iraq. At his request, a meeting with the Bedouin Chiefs was arranged in their tent.

When he came back to India he heard that his only grandson had passed away in Germany. News reached that Gandhiji had started in Yerabda Jail, Poona, a fast unto death. Tagore sent him a congratulatory telegram. Later, when the fast was broken, he was at Gandhiji's side at whose request he sang from Gitanjali: "When the heart is dry and parched...come (thou) with a burst of songs."

Next year Tagore delivered Kamala Lectures at the University of Calcutta. He spoke in Bengali, in *Manusher Dharma.* This was a shorter and better version of his Oxford lectures. It was followed by a gay musical satire on a stereotyped society and a play, *Chandalika,* an adaptation from the Buddhist legends. It is the story of an outcaste girl falling in love with a disciple of the Buddha at whose intervention tragedy is averted.

Tagore was again out on a fund raising tour. He gave a lecture at the Andhra University, Waltair, on "Man." Then he went to Hyderabad. Earlier the Nizam had donated some money for Islamic studies at the Visva-Bharati. After a brief visit to Bombay he came back to Calcutta, where he spoke on Rammohan whom he called "Bharat-Pathik" (Pilgrim of the Indian Way). Jawaharlal Nehru paid a short visit to Santiniketan where his daughter, Indira was studying. Next followed by the Convocation Address at Banaras Hindu University and a visit to Lahore.

By this time the mud-house, "Shyamali," which he hoped would be his "last house," was put up and decorated with the help of Santiniketan artists. But he had, later, to move to other houses nearby and Shyamali still stands, a lovely, abandoned apparition. In 1936 he addressed an Education Conference in Calcutta in which he pleaded for a Home University scheme. His own Visva-Bharati began a Lok Siksha Samsad. Soon he made another fund-raising trip to North India, Patna, Allahabad, Lahore and Delhi. Mahatma Gandhi met him with a begging bowl. He enquired about Visva-Bharati's deficit. At his behest an anonymous donor sent a cheque. The poet came back to Visva-Bharati.

He addressed the Calcutta University's Convocation Address in Bengali leaving aside the convention of speeches in English. On April 15, 1937 Jawaharlal Nehru inaugurated the China Bhavan for Sino-Indian Studies at Santiniketan with Tan Yan-Shan as its Director. Then Rabindranath published two books *Chharhar Chhabi*, a book on folk poems and *Visva-Parichaya*, a primer on science. Now age was creeping slowly and he paid a farewell visit to his estate at Patisar (now in Bangladesh). Even then he spoke out against the government's inhuman treatment of political prisoners in the Andamans. "In September 1937 he composed and directed *Varsha-Mangal*, a song and dance sequence celebrating the rainy season, which was staged in Calcutta, with him seated on the stage."[16]

On the evening of 10 September, 1937, while talking he felt unconscious. Fortunately he recovered his consciousness, the borderland experience left traces behind. *Prantik* (The Borderland) was a new book, death-haunted. Then he spent some restful months at Mongpu at Darjeeling under the loving care of Maitreyi Devi, a young poetess. When the Sino-Japanese war broke out, Tagore was deeply hurt.

He wrote a letter to the Japanese poet, Yone Noguchi protesting against the Japanese aggression.

The international situation became deteriorated. On September 1, 1939 the Second World War was declared. The Indian leaders' request to declare Indian independence before the war was turned down by Britain. For Christmas service at Santiniketan Tagore wrote:

> Those who struck Him once
> in the name of their rulers
> are born again in the present age.
> They gather in their prayer halls in a pious garb,
> they call their soldiers,
> "Kill, kill," they shout.
> In their roaring mingles the music of their hymns,
> while the son of Man in His agony prays,
> "O God, fling, fling far away
> this cup filled with the bitterest of poisons."[17]

On February 17, 1940 Gandhiji and Kasturba came to Santiniketan. Tagore handed over to Gandhiji a brief letter pleading for the preservation of Visva-Bharati, "the vessel carrying the cargo of his life's best treasure." On August 7, 1940, the Oxford University conferred on him, at Santiniketan itself, D. Litt. (*honoris causa*). The body was ailing but the mind still alert. He wrote two short stories, "Laboratory" and "Badnam" (Bad name) which are modern with a vengeance. The old hill resort of Kalimpong did not improve his health. He was bed-ridden for the next few months.

But he produced Rogsajyay (sick bed) and Arogya (Recovery) which were tired, reticent, gerontic and self-critical, almost merciless in their self-analysis. On March 12, 1941 his last birthday address, "Crisis in Civilisation" was read out from a wheel chair. A few days later, "a representative of the court of Tripura conferred upon him the title of Bharat Bhaskar (Sun of India)."[18]

Lastly, he had to undergo a surgery and on 25 July, 1941 he was taken to Calcutta. Too weak to write, he dictated two terrible poems. "Sorrows Dark Night" and "Thou Guileful One." These give a new focus on his life and works. The operation was not a success. On 7 August, 1941 at midday he passed away. Ready for the event, the poet had earlier written a song to be sung at his death:

> In front lies the ocean of peace,
> launch the boat, Helmsman,
> you will be the comrade ever....[19]

It was as though an age had come to an end. But who was he? Did he know, does anyone?

> "The first day's Sun
> asked
> at the new manifestation of being —
> Who are you?
> No answer came.
> Year after year went by,
> the last Sun of the day
> the last question utters
> on the western seashore,
> in the silent evening —
> Who are you?
> He gets no answer."[20]

Ages hence the question will echo and re-echo to tease generations unborn and receive no answer. The sun had set.

A man of genius is as much moulded by the age he lives in, as he in his turn, shapes the times. A novelist is essentially a social being and must be an extrovert while a novel is a social product. Tagore lived in times when the forces of the Indian Renaissance were asserting themselves in all directions. They were the days of conflict between the old and the new, of rebellion against tradition and reaction against modernity, of political upheaval, social reforms and cultural renaissance. His novels, being the imaginative reconstructions of reality, reflect the working of these forces. In them Tagore presented two basic ideals : the Indian national consciousness, the Upanishadic ideal of universal man, the enlightened soul; and the typical Indian Woman, symbolising the sensibility and energy of the *Prakriti.* In fact, the age was one of the most turbulent in Indian history and Tagore played a crucial role in both reflecting and moulding the intellectual, social, and cultural climate in resurgent Bengal. Deeply conscious of the decadence in Indian ethos, he responded readily to the rationalistic, humanistic, and literary influences of the West, brought in by the British advent, and ushered in a new era in Indian letters. I shall in this last part of the chapter, analyse how Tagore wrote his novels with the promotion of liberal humanism in life and thought, the development of prose as an artistic medium and the induction of social, political and psychological issues as literary themes. I shall also broadly examine these novels in point of thematic concerns, analysis, and structural technique.

Tagore stood the central figure in the Indian Renaissance. With his extraordinary nexus of talents and gifts as poet, playwright, philosopher, painter, composer, novelist, short story writer, educationist, culture hero and reconciler of indigenous and foreign traditions has been rightly hailed as "the Leonardo da Vinci of the Indian Renaissance."[21] Tagore succeeded in infusing a spirit of liberal humanism into the life of his times. The values informing his art and life are derived from the very springs of humaneness and are not invalidated by the experience of the contemporary man and his obsessional preoccupation with existential questions. His work may be said to have brought a new signification to the perennially profound issues confronting man in the metaphysical, cultural, social, and political spheres.

As a living legend of his own lifetime, Tagore projected an image of his personality in which the myth and the man seemed inseparable. A keen aliveness to the happenings around him was one of his strong points and he exhibited to the end of his life a deep interest in all matters concerning his country and the world at large. In his novels he delineates the inner landscape of Indian experience at one of the crucial moments of her history. In them he projects a society in transition. They represent his deepest concerns about the emerging social order in his country.

His novels deal with social problems of a fundamental nature : the woeful conditions of Hindu widows and the emergence of a new type of woman in quest of self-fulfilment as in *Binodini*, the struggle for values in one's own tradition as in *Gora*, the conflict between true and false patriotism as in *The Home and the World*, problems of love versus possession as in *Two Sisters* and *The Garden*, and the futility and tragedy of political terrorism as in *Four-Chapters*—in fact, a whole complex of conflicts and cross-currents in contemporary Indian life which could not be framed in theological terms.

Tagore's novels symbolize his perspectivisation of the social scene in India emphasising on humanistic values. The humanistic persuasion dealt with in his novels is directed towards a change in die-hard reading of the Indian traditions to facilitate the birth of a new order. Mulk Raj Anand, himself a humanist of note, remarked that Tagore was one of the greatest humanists of our country and the world who taught whole generations of the country to be humanists. Tagore loved man so fervently that he believed, there is nothing in creation higher than the spirit of man. Even God has to manifest Himself through man:

> "The revealment of the Infinite in the finite, which is the motive of all creation, is not seen in its perfection in the starry heavens, in the beauty of the flowers. It is in the soul of man."[22]

Tagore opined that humanism which places man in the centre of things could form the basis for reforming the Hindu Society by itself. Born at a time when the nation itself was involved in a process of rebirth, Tagore inherited the spirit of the Indian Renaissance and later strove his utmost to consolidate its foundations through "the Hindu-British symbiosis." There was a headlong rush for Westernisation mixconstrued as modernisation among the educated young Bengal group of the late twenties of the nineteenth century. They attempted at an outright condemnation of everything Indian. But Raja Rammohan Roy, according to R.N. Tagore, accepted the West without renouncing the East, and single handed, brought the new Bengal into being. Very soon old customs, ideas, beliefs and institutions became subject to rational scrutiny and the process of reformation of a fossilised, convention-ridden and largely sacredotal social system was inaugurated by Raja Rammohan Roy, Iswar Chandra Vidyasagar and others. An attitude of self-analysis and willingness to integrate Western values with the ancient traditions of India was fostered, resulting in institutions like the *Brahmo Samaj* (1828). But the orthodox Hindus began a counter-offensive under the leadership of Raja Radhakanta Deb who started the *Dharma Sabha* in 1830. Then came out two opposing attitudes—"the reformist liberal humanism as symbolised in Tagore's novels in Paresh Babu and Anandamoyi in *Gora* or even agnosticism as seen in uncle Jagmohan in *Chaturanga*, and the romantic nostalgia for the glories of the past and efforts for a neo-Hindu revival as witnessed in the career of Gora."[23]

Tagore's novels hold up a mirror to this society in conflict and reflect the crisis of spirit resulting from the dialectal relationship between the reformist and revivalist impulses.

Tagore himself strove for a synthesis of the past and the present, the Eastern and the Western viewpoints. It is important to remember that he was a reformer and not a revolutionary and was not for the abandonment of tradition but for its reformation by removing the acretions of ages. That is why he remains true to Indian tradition or all that is acceptable in it while portraying the emergence of modern sensibility. That is why his novels—*Binodini, The Wreck or Two Sisters* stress the need for a social change but stop short of a radical transformation.

The Western impact on India initiated a new vernacular prose style. The efforts of William Carey and his associates in devising Bengali typescript and the bringing out of stories, dialogues, essays, dictionaries, and grammatical handbooks in Bengali resulted in the popularisation of a standardised prose style which gained a new charm and flavour later in the hands of Raja Rammohan Roy, Iswar Chandra Vidyasagar, and Debendranath Tagore. Among the books published by Carey was *Raja Pratapaditya Charita* (by Ramram Basu) was the first historical novel in Bengal. The brief but momentous existence of Fort William College (1800-1854) was like an "Oxford of the East." The efforts of the scholars of this college acquired an enlarged base and an extended range as a result of the attempts made by the enterprising writers like Michael Madhusudan Dutt, Henry Derozio, Ramesh Chunder Dutt, Bankim Chandra Chatterjee, etc.

Peary Chand Mitra's *Alaler Gharer Dulal* (The Spoilt Child of a Rich Family) which appeared in book form in 1858 and Kaliprasanna Sinha's *Hutom Pyacar Naksa* (Sketches by Hutom the Owl) which started in 1862 mark a crucial stage towards the appearance of the novel as both have contemporary settings and employ a colloquial prose style. When the novel first appeared in an integrated form, it took the shape of historical fiction. Bankim's *Durgeshnandini* (1865) is an example. Krishna Kripalani and T.W. Clark opine that Bankim was the first Bengali novelist. But Mulk Raj Anand has differed from this view and has designated Rabindranath Tagore as "the first novelist in India."[24] In fact, Tagore, in terms of theme and technique could be hailed as the Father of Modern Indian Novel.

Bankim is a romancer extending the old myth and legend of India. His historical romances suggest an inadequate appreciation of the contemporary situation and a precarious grasp of the novel form. A convert to the spirit of neo-Hindu revivalism Bankim projects a fictional world of an idealised with out-of-ordinary incidents and larger-than-life characters. His *Durgesnandini* (1865), *Kapalkundala* (1866), *Raj Singh* (1883), and *Devi Chaudhurani* (1884) exemplify, in both form and content, the medieval romances offering little criticism of the life of the times.

Even *Anandmath* (1882) does not successfully define the principal situation because of the author's eagerness to perpetuate old values as a result of which the characters lapse into just ideational abstract figures. *Brishbriksha* (1873) and *Krishnakanter Vil* (1878) are novels in which the characters are not sharply individualised and delineated with any degree of psychological subtlety. The characters lack complexity and reveal no inward changes, observable for the first time in Indian fiction in Tagore's *Binodini* (1903). The piling up of incidents in an attempt to sustain the story interest does not result in the realisation of the character's predicament in meaningful terms. Bankim's fiction consists of historical romance exhibiting little concern about the contemporary reality or about the developing Indian personality. Mulk Raj Anand remarks that the credit for creating modern novel must go to Rabindranath Tagore.

His distinction as a novelist lies in his creation of the modern novel form which is forward looking and manifesting an imaginative comprehension of the central issues confronting the Indian society of the time. He was concerned with many of the problems of the newly unfolding India—self-government, self-reliance, the status of women, the role of tradition, rural reconstruction, national education and the intercultural synthesis of East and West. He had identified himself with the forces of rationalism and reformation. His novels project a humanism born of an acute awareness of the betrayal of human personality engineered by the powers of stagnation and rigid orthodoxy. "His novels stress the needs for promotion of catholicism in human relations and dealings and prevention of the erosion of human dignity while creating conditions for the realisation of self-actualisation, if not self-fulfilment."[25] This is specially true of his women characters struggling against their dehumanization in the name of tradition. He assigns a central place to women in his novels because their roles are crucial to any transformation of Indian ethos. A spirit of realism runs through the novels of Tagore. He sought realistic models of presentation by avoiding romantic posturing or attitudinising.

Coming to the variety of themes figuring in his novels it can be said that he seems to take interest in the tensions, conflicts, contradictions, frustrations, and embarrassments stemming from the polarities of tradition and modernity, past and present, orthodoxy and radicalism; and idealism and opportunism. His novels spanning half a century—his first novels, *Bau Thakuranir Hat* (The Young Queen's Market), published in 1883, and the last novel, *Char Adhyay* (Four Chapters), appearing in 1934, cover an epoch-making era of Indian history *i.e.* late nineteenth and early twentieth centuries. His novels deal with concrete human situations to provide a searching analysis of the position obtaining in Indian society. V.S. Naravane explains:

> "Tagore the novelist, like Tagore the philosopher, recognises that man has in him an Infinite as well as a finite element; and that, nobility, love and calmness are as 'real' as depravity, hatred and tension. He, therefore, creates people who have the same passions, foibles and frailties that we have, but who can surprise us by flashes of profound wisdom or by acts of supreme self-sacrifice."[26]

Tagore's novels reflect a vision of India caught up in the cross-currents of opposing ideologies, of the questioning of the old or traditional moral sanctions in search of self-fulfilment, the clash between the reformist and revivalist forces, the conflict between the moderate and extremist elements in politics as well as the eternal struggle in the human consciousness between love and sacrifice. He derived the popular brand of patriotism, based on emotionalism and chauvinism. He held that independence could be achieved only by the promotion of self-help and strength. And sacrifice and service are the only true tests of strength. The two novels, *The Home and the World* and *Four Chapters* embody the above theme though the main interest in both is in the human rather than political situation. Nikhil and to a certain extent, Bimala in the first novel and the two lovers, Ela and Atin in the second novel face suffering and tragedy by being caught up in the convulsions of political struggles. The novel *Gora* upholds the ideal of the synthesis of races, religions and cultures.

The three novels, *Binodini, The Wreck* and *Chaturanga* relate to some of the pressing social issues which rocked the Bengali Hindu society towards the end of the last century. *Binodini* dramatises the struggle of a young, beautiful widow for self-actualisation and selfhood in a social system that denies all scope for such attempts. *The Wreck*, as Anand remarks, is "a model of presentation of the new conflict of values that arose in Indian society through the contrast of the hedonistic idea of marriage as against the old Indian idea of marriage by arrangement."[27] *Chaturanga* explores the moral and spiritual dilemma generated by the counteraction of scientific rationalism on the one hand and the resurgent Hindu religiosity on the other, as projected in the career of Sachis.

The three novellas, namely, *Two Sisters, The Garden and Farewell, My Friend*, are psychological studies without political or social overtones. *Two Sisters* is premised on the dual image of woman as mother and beloved and deals with the tensions created by the triangular relationships of a husband, his devoted wife and the wife's sister who is drawn to the husband. The emotional entanglement is resolved by the younger sister's sacrifice and withdrawal and the novel ends on a happy note. Quite the reverse happens in *The Garden,* where the heroine becomes too possessive of her husband's love and in spite of illness and impending death, cannot countenance another woman's love for him. Drained of her capacity for love and generosity, she inflicts untold misery on herself and others and falls a victim to a violent paroxysm of jealousy which proves fatal. *Farewell, My Friend,* a playful mockery of romanticised love describes the coming together and parting of two lovers in the Arcadian surroundings of a hill-station, Shillong but whose idealised love cannot withstand the onset of reality. They go their separate ways, bidding fond farewells to each other in verse.

Though Tagore tackles a wide variety of themes in his novels, his characters are confined to a narrow segment of society, that of the upper-middle class. A predominantly urban milieu forms a kind of unchanging setting for all his novels. Moreover, the locale of all the novels is Bengal, which being the radiating centre of the new ideological and cultural configurations, stood for the entire nation itself. "What Bengal thinks today, all India thinks tomorrow" was undoubtedly true of the times of Indian renaissance and Reformation. It is the upper class Bengali Hindu Intellectuals who pioneered the new political, social, cultural and literary movements in the country, and hence, Tagore's projection of the social scene in Bengal has an all-India significance.

Tagore's male characters have a representative nature. His young heroes a whole galaxy of contemporary Indian portraits, remain in our memory as the poignant symbols of fighters who fell in the all-embracing manifold struggle of our generation to find a new way of life. The tangled relationships among the characters appear as an index of their faltering perception or inadequate moral sense. In this regard G.V. Raj comments: "The cultural or social impasse that the characters confront affords an opportunity for the testing of human personality and its resourcefulness."[28]

Tagore's heroines display a rare assurance and psychological strength. Through a variety of perspectives, Tagore depicts their search for identity or realisation of self-fulfilment within the bounds of tradition and society. Edward Thompson, commenting on Tagore's outlook on woman in Indian society, remarks: "he would have her remain woman—a centre of love and inspiration without which the world is poverty-stricken. But he has never ceased to attack the injustice and cruelty which regard woman as inferior or unfitted for education or arts."[29] Thus, while conveying the feelings of tenderness and devotion, traditionally associated with Indian womanhood, he depicts their struggle against discrimination and ill usage, as can be seen from *Binodini, Gora* and *Chaturanga*. These characters are never static and do not remain mere products of artistic control or manipulation.

In the sphere of Tagore's architectonics, we can say that his novels suffer from a certain weakness of craftsmanship, a flabbiness of narrative. It shows an inadequate appreciation of the relative importance of cause and effect in the fictional rendering of experience. The undue reliance on chance and coincidence in some of the novels and the contrived endings of some others point towards an impatience on the part of the novelist in working out a structure of ordered episodes.

Though not a real experimentalist Tagore introduced some new fictional techniques. The use of flashback by Tagore in the structuring of his narrative is a new thing. The employment of multiple points of view (as in *The Home and The World*) and "central consciousness" (as in *Chaturanga*) does invest them with a kind of psychological realism not found in Bankim's novels. The first person narrative technique though not invariably successful, does help him in eliminating authorial intervention which is what his predecessor has not been able to accomplish. His heavy reliance on dialogue to intensify the dramatic effect of his novels is also another instance of his innovative bias.

Several scenes from his novels seem fit for stage representation, needing no adaptation whatsoever. The dialogues in his novels are marked by a dramatic verse and poetic grace besides naturalness which invests the fictional frames with life. This is not unexpected in a writer who is also a playwright of equal merit.

Tagore remains a pioneer in initiating the psychological novel based on social reality and in bringing out the nuances of change in his major characters through their interaction with circumstance. His novels mark the transition from the tradition of historical romance which characterised the Indian novel upto his time to the realistic tradition that has set in with him. It is Tagore who ushered in the spirit of social realism and liberal humanism into the Indian novel and it is to him that the modern Indo-Anglian novel owes its moral and human concern in its projection of contemporary reality. Tagore as a realistic analyst of social relationship has written novel on the themes formed out of the matrix of social and emotional life. He is the first novelist introducing the themes such as—the predicament of the Indian woman, the clash between the orthodox and the progressive, the right consciousness of national heritage, and the conflict of values in a changing life style. Tagore wrote thirteen novels in all of which nine were translated into English. Professor Humayun Kabir remarks that Tagore lifted the Bengali novel from its narrow social environment and gave it a character of universal acceptability.

REFERENCES

1. Buddhadeva Bose, *An Acre of Green Grass* (Calcutta: Papyrus, 1948; rpt. 1982), 15.
2. K.R. Srinivasa Iyengar, *Rabindranath Tagore : A Critical Introduction* (New Delhi: Sterling Publishers Pvt. Ltd., 1987), 4.
3. Quoted in Sisirkumar Ghose, *Rabindranath Tagore* (New Delhi: Sahitya Akademi, 1986, rpt. 1994), 12.
4. *Ibid.*, 12.
5. *Ibid.*, 12.

6. Probhat Kumar Mukherji, *Life of Tagore*, (New Delhi: Hind Pocket Books, 1977), 57.
7. Quoted in Sisirkumar Ghose, *Rabindranath Tagore* (New Delhi: Sahitya Akademi, 1994), 15.
8. *Ibid.*, 15.
9. *Ibid.*, 17.
10. *Ibid.*, 19.
11. Probhat Kumar Mukherji, *Life of Tagore* (New Delhi: Hind Pocket Books, 1977), 150.
12. Sisirkumar Ghose, *Rabindranath Tagore*, (New Delhi: Sahitya Akademi, 1986), 21.
13. *Ibid.*, 23.
14. *Ibid.*, 24.
15. Ibid., 25.
16. Krishna Kripalani, *Rabindranath Tagore: A Biography* (Calcutta: Visva-Bharati Publishing Department, 1980), 413.
17. *Ibid.*, 424.
18. Probhat Kumar Mukherjee, *Life of Tagore* (Delhi: Hind Pocket Books, 1977), 257.
19. Quoted in Krishna Kripalani, *Rabindranath Tagore: A Biography* (Calcutta: Visva-Bharati Publishing Dept., 1980), 452.
20. *Ibid.*, 450.
21. Niharranjan Ray, "Three Novels of Tagore." "Chokher Bali, Gora, Yogayoga," *Indian Literature*, Vol. 4, 1961, 164.
22. Rabindranath Tagore, *Sadhana* (1913, rpt. Madras: Macmillan, 1979), 34.
23. G.V. Raj, *Tagore: The Novelist* (New Delhi: Sterling Publishers Pvt. Ltd., 1983), 6.
24. *Ibid.*, 8.
25. *Ibid.*, 11.
26. V.S. Naravane, *An Introduction to Rabindranath Tagore* (Delhi: The Macmillan Company of India Ltd., 1977), 115.
27. Mulk Raj Anand, "Modern Indian Fiction," in *Indian Annual Review*, 1954 (New Delhi: Information Service of India, 1954), 193.
28. G.V. Raj, *Tagore: The Novelist* (New Delhi: Sterling Publishers Pvt. Ltd., 1983), 15.
29. Edward Thomson, *Rabindranath Tagore: His Life and Works*, rev. by Kalidas Nag (Calcutta: Y.M.C.A. Publishing House, 1961), 74-75.

2

General Definition, Interpretation and Characteristics of Humanism and Nationalism

To define and interpret humanism is not an easy task as the history of humanism is long and involved. It has also been entertaining several and diverse connotations. But many humanists have so far tried to define and interpret it starting with an allusion to the famous Greek philosopher Protagoras's dictum — "Man is the measure of all things." This dictum admits of no distinction between sense and reason in its simple interpretation. W.T. Stace interprets the dictum as:

> "Man is the measure of all things"; certainly, but man as a rational being, not man as a bundle of particular sensations, subjective impressions, impulses, irrational prejudices, self-will, mere eccentricities, oddities, foibles, and fancies.[1]

Thus with Protagoras Greek philosophy turned from theology and cosmology to man. It sowed the seed of humanism which was to grow up into a huge tree of myriad ramifications through the lively interpretations of great humanists.

Next the great Greek humanist Socrates interpreted humanism through his axiom "Know thyself". His humanism really lay in his philosophy conjoining man with the eternal, and this through the right knowledge which is virtue. Because to him virtue, knowledge and human happiness were all identieal. Right knowledge ought to lead man to right action, and right action to unsullied happiness. Hence he pleaded for the acquisition of the knowledge of one's self.

Plato's humanism lay in his ethics of the establishment of proper balance between reason, spirit and desire. Man arrives at virtue when reason controls and guides him to knowledge. Thus in the ethical teachings of both Socrates and Plato human well-being occupies the central position.

According to Aristotle, reason is man's highest attribute and his glory. Man must be viewed neither as angel nor as devil but as man. And the virtue we must study is human virtue. Herschell Baker, commenting on Aristotle's humanism, remarks: "His (Aristotle's) is the most urbane kind of humanism, one that candidly names as its object an attainable good."[2] In the same book Herschell Baker sums up the Greek view of humanism in the following words:

> "To understand his own morphology as well as that of the universe is man's highest function, and leads to the state of well-being which is virtue.
>
> This is the apogee of humanism—which, for the Greek, was an attitude and habit of mind rather than a philosophical system or cult."[3]

In classical Greek literature like *Illiad* the strain of humanism is seen in the pathos resulting from man's struggle against the inevitable cosmic forces. Indeed, the ancient Greek humanism shows profound respect for man. This can be justified with the Sophoclean adage: "Wonders are many, and none is more wonderful than man."

Renaissance humanism may be interpreted as an intellectual impulse, a cultural and educational programme for the moulding of a desirable type of man in the fashion of the man glorified in the classics, which revealed a magnificent civilization built by the ancient Greeks and Romans who enjoyed happy lives for centuries without any assistance from revelation or supernatural sanctions. This led the Renaissance man's attention to the question of how best he could make his earthly life a joyful life instead of to the problem of what might become of him after death. Renaissance humanism dwells on classicism. Humanism here means the study of "humane letters." This involved an act of self-expression through the editing and translation of the ancient Greek and Latin classics with them as models. Here we cite the works of Petrarch the inaugurator and "the prototype embodiment of the rising zeal for classical study."[4] Petrarch's philosophy involved the teaching of the art of living well and happily. A host of humanists—Boccaccio, Salutati, Bruni, Poggio, Pomponazzi, Lorenzo Valla, Ficino, and Mirandola followed the tract of Petrarch.

Of the Christian, humanists mention may be made of Erasmus, the prince of the modern humanists. His philosophy dwells on the change-over from scientific questions to the problems of moral life and religious imagination. He emphasized on the dignity of man through Christ's atonement and God's grace. In him the new spirit of European humanism found its expression. In his book, *Praise of Folly,* a Voltairean satire, he exposed and criticized the corrupt church, depraved clergy and sterile scholastics. He insisted on the importancc of the life of integrity and understanding and practice of true Christianity free from superstition and dogma.

Among the modern humanists F.C.S. Schiller (1864-1937) is very prominent. He branded pragmatism as humanism. He believed in the pragmatic criterion of truth. Human experience is essentially dynamic and is the sole criterion of truth. Transempirical or non-human truth is meaningless. Schiller's pragmatic humanism aims at rehumanizing philosophy to energize it to undertake its highest task, the service of man.

In the contemporary world naturalistic humanism, also called "scientific humanism" has gained tremendous popularity. It is also called "applied naturalism" as it is so closely related to naturalism. Repudiating all forms of supernaturalism it holds that man is a wholly natural creature whose well-being rests on his own efforts unaided by transcendental support. It strongly rejects the illusion of immortality and is content with the life here and now. It is against the existence of God and the need of religion. The famous naturalistic humanist Corliss Lamont summarizing his viewpoints writes thus:

> Humanism is the viewpoint that man has but one life to lead and should make the most of it in terms of creative work and happiness; that human happiness is its own justification and requires no sanction or support from supernatural sources; that in the form of heavenly gods or immortal heavens, does not exist; and that human beings, using their own intelligence and co-operating with one another, can build an enduring citadel of peace and beauty upon this earth....
>
> The Humanist philosophy persistently strives to remind men that their only home is in the mundane world. There is no use of searching elsewhere for happiness and fulfilment, for there is no place else to go. We human beings must find our destiny and our promised land in the here and now, or not at all.[5]

One important division of naturalistic humanism is religious humanism. Its adherents vehemently oppose the ideas of original Sin and human depravity, and they define God (and religion) so strangely that He has been surreptitiously removed from the scene.

Another form of humanism is "evolutionary humanism" or "transhumanism" propounded by Julian Huxley. It originates from Huxley's belief in the Darwinian theory of evolution. Man is the latest product of the evolutionary process and so he is a part of nature. Now, man is the sole agent of the further progress of evolution. Huxley believes that art and science are two aspects of the same reality and therefore they can have meaning only if they serve the common goal of man's happiness. In fact, evolutionary humanism is a new religion which Huxley proposes for the benefit of the entire mankind.

One important form of humanism is Maritain's theological humanism based on Catholic thought. Other forms of humanism are Sartre's existentialist humanism and Irving Babbit's academic humanism.

Though we cannot equate Buddhism with humanism, Buddha himself may be seen as a sort of humanist. His Eight fold path of right action and right thought is directed to the cure of human sorrow. So he was concretely concerned with man. Compassion or tenderness is the core of Buddha's humanism.

Some other forms of humanism propounded by the medieval Hindu saints and saints of Islam and Sikhs were mainly attempts at elevating the downtrodden by preaching the brotherhood and equality of men and by pleading for a casteless society.

Raja Ram Mohan Roy's humanism consists of his fight against the evil aspects of Hinduism. He emphasised on having a universal religion to be embraced by the whole mankind.

Mahatma Gandhiji's humanism, slightly different from Tagore's humanism, had a profounder mass appeal because of Mahatma's dedicated devotion to the cause of the downtrodden. The common aspect of Gandhi's humanism and Tagore's humanism is the presence of mystical and religious bias. Commenting on the humanism of Gandhi and Tagore Dr. V.S. Naravane remarks:

> They were both humanists, Gandhi's humanism had a moral-social basis, while Tagore's was coloured by his aesthetic mystical experience; but both were firm believers in the worth and dignity of the human individual.[6]

Another form of humanism is M.N. Roy's radical or scientific humanism based on democratic revolution. This is an alternative to communism. He believed in the democratic society founded on radical humanism.

Mulk Raj Anand's humanism is comprehensive historical humanism. It develops from his intense preoccupation with the whole man. His writings are inspired by his love of man and he writes:

> And as my media as a writer were the memory and

> imagination, the substance of my work became the whole man, and the whole gamut of human relationships, rather than only on single part of it.[7]

So the central concern of humanism is man. Its aim is the achievement of man's happiness by recognising the dignity of man as man.

HUMANISM AS THEME OF NOVELS BY THE GREAT INDO-ANGLIAN NOVELISTS AND R.N. TAGORE

This humanism has been a recurrent theme of the novels of many great Indo-Anglian novelists like Mulk Raj Anand, Raja Rao, R.K. Narayan, Arun Joshi, Chaman Nahal, Manohar Malgonkar, Nayantara Sahgal, Kamala Markandaya, Ruth Prawer Jhavbala, Anita Desai, Salman Rusdie and a host of other novelists. Apart from these novelists, R.N. Tagore dealt with this theme on a wider scale in some of his novels. His humanism involves his universality and sense of identity with all men and his revolt against all types of tyranny and injustice.

Tagore deals with the theme of humanism in his novels—*Binodini, The Wreck* and *Chaturanga* by relating them to some of the pressing social human issues of his time; and *Two Sisters, The Garden* and *Farewell, My Friend* by making them psychological studies. Each of these novels is discussed in detail in the next chapter (chapter 3) in a chronological order of publication.

In spite of many attempts which have been made to define "nationalism" in literature, there has not been any clear-cut definition of this term so far. Even famous books, exclusively written on nationalism like K.R. Minogue's *Nationalism* and Hans Kohn's *Nationalism: Its Meaning and History*, do not attempt any such definition. About nationalism K.R. Minogue writes: "The concept of nationalism was alien to India before the nineteenth century just as it was alien to all other Asian and African countries."[8] Rabinaranath Tagore also observes: "This idea dawned upon the Indian horizon in the nineteenth century as an impact of and as a reaction to the British colonial rule in

India."[9] Nationalism was adopted as a weapon for winning freedom from European imperialism and colonial regime in India and other Asian and African countries. Even in the West the concept of nationalism was comparatively new. It had its birth only in the later eighteenth century France at the time of the French Revolution. People took "nationalism not as a vehicle of individual liberty but as adoration of collective power."[10]

NATIONALISM AS THEME OF NOVELS BY THE GREAT INDO-ANGLIAN NOVELISTS AND R.N. TAGORE

We may define and interpret nationalism through its growth in India as reflected in the novels by the Indo-Anglian writers. In fact, the Indo-Anglian fiction has reflected the various aspects of this nationalism. One aspect of nationalism as shown in the early Indo-Anglian novels is the spirit of self-identification or self-assertion. Interpreting this aspect of nationalism K.R. Minogue remarks: "When the people of a country living under an autocratic or oppressive rule, very often foreign, want to throw off that rule and establish a new political setup of their own choice, the people of that country are said to have been imbued with the spirit of nationalism."[11] The native people, in their zeal to show that they are by no means inferior to their rulers, make a search for their own identity and try to affirm it. The superiority complex of the rulers incite them to assert themselves. There are very fine reflections of this kind of self-assertion in Indo-Anglian novels grouped into two as—(1) the documentary novels and stories depicting Indian life and traditions, manners and customs and (2) the collections of Indian folk tales, mythological tales, and legends.

Important novels belonging to the first group are—*Govinda Samanta* by Lal Behari Day (1874); *The Young Zemindar* by Sochee Chunder Dutt (1885); *Sarala and Hingana* by Khetrapal Chakarvarti as one volume of fiction (1896), etc. To the second group belong *The Dive for Death* (1911) by T. Ramakrishna Pillai; Dwijendra Nath Neogi's *Sacred Tales of India* (1916); *True Tales of Indian Life* (1917) and *Anecdotes of Indian Life* (1920);

Humayun Kabir's *Men and Rivers* (1945); Lal Behari Day's *The Folk Tales of Bengal* (1883); *Tales of Bengal* (1926) and *Folk Stories of Bengal* (1944); Purendu Narayan Sinha's *Chandi or the Great Plan* (1922); Dewan Sharar's *Hindu Fairy Tales* (1936), etc.

Another aspect of nationalism reflected in Indo-Anglian novels is the glorification of the past for the same purpose of self-assertion or probing into the past for drawing lessons for the present. The discovery of the past through historical fiction for achieving unity or self-determination among the people of a country may be interpreted as one of the meanings of nationalism. In this regard prof. G.P. Sarma makes a relevant remark as—"Behind the search for the past glories of a country by its people lies a national spirit."[12] This spirit is the sign of first stage of the development of nationalism. And K.R. Minogue also remarks that through historical fiction the people of a country want to rouse a "political and historical consciousness of the nation."[13]

Important fiction reflecting this aspect of nationalism are Sochee Chunder Dutt's *The Time of Yore* (1885); K.K. Sinha's *Sanjogita* (1903); *Padmini* (1903) by T. Ramakrishna; *Nur Jahan* (1909) by Sirdar Jogendra Singh; A. Madhaviah's *Clarinda* (1915); A.S. Panchapakesa Ayyar's *Baladitya* (1930) and *Three Men of Destiny* (1939); S. Gopalan's *Old Tanjore* (1938); Joseph Furtado's *Golden Goa* (1938); etc.

Another meaning of nationalism may be the reforming zeal of the people for a better and happier society and a stronger nation. The attempt of seeking freedom from foreign oppression also wants at the same time to organise and consolidate the collective power of the people by removing social injustices and age-old evil practices. This attempt is a national process. This endeavour involves consolidation and integration of various peoples into a race or nation. The Indo-Anglian novels and stories with a reformative purpose may be treated as having a nationalistic bias.

Important novels and stories of this category are—K.K. Sinha's *The Star of Sikri* (1893); Lady Krupabai Satthianandhan's *Kamala: A Story of Hindu Life* (1894) and *Saguna: A Story of Native Christian Life* (1895); Shevantibai Nikambe's *Ratnabai* (1895); Cornelia Sorabji's short stories—*Love and Life Behind the Purdah* (1901), *Sun Babies* (1904) and *Between the Twilights* (1908) and her novel, *Shubala: A Child Mother* (1920); Sirdar Jogendra Singh's three novels—*Narsin* (1911), *Kamla* (1925), and *Kamini* (1931); A Madhaviah's novel *Thillai Govindan* (1916) and his short stories—*Short Stories by "Kusika"* (1916); Bal Krishna's novel *The Love of Kusuma* (1910); Mulk Raj Anand's *Untouchable* (1935); *Coolie* (1936); *Two Leaves and a Bud* (1937); *The Village* (1939); *Across the Black Waters* (1940); *The Sword and the Sickle* (1942); *The Big Heart* (1945); his short stories—*The Lost Child and Other Stories* (1934); *A Lament on the Death of a Master of Arts* (1939); *The Barber's Trade Union and Other Stories* (1944); *The Tractor and Corn Goddess* (1947); R.K. Narayan's *Swami and Friends* (1935); *The Bachelor of Arts* (1937); *The Dark Room* (1938); *The English Teacher* (1949); his short stories—*Dodu and Other Stories* (1943), *Malgudi Days* (1943); *Cyclone and Other Stories* (1944) and *An Astrologer's Day and Other Stories* (1947); Louise Gracius's Short Stories—*Wild Winds* (1940) and *Eastern Clay* (1948); Ahmed Ali's famous novel *Twilight in Delhi* (1940); D.F. Karaka's three novels—*Just Flesh* (1941); *There Lay the City* (1942) and *We Never Die* (1944); Manjeri S. Isvaran's short stories—*Naked Shingles* (1941); *Shiva Ratri* (1943); *Angry Dust* (1944); *Rikshawalla* (1946) and *Fancy Tales* (1947); Ela Sen's stories—*Darkening Days* (1944); Iqbalunnisa Hussain's novel *Purdah and Polygamy* (1944); etc.

One important aspect of nationalism is the political aspect. Nationalism may be defined as the attempt or struggle for political freedom. In India freedom movement can be divided into three phases. Three categories of Indo-Anglian political novels and stories reflect the spirit and movement of these three phases. The first phase involves spontaneous, unorganised armed rebellions against the newly established British rule. The second phase involves the demand for self-government for Indians while the English educated Indians still expressing their willingness to remain under the British Empire itself. The third phase expresses Indian people's demand for complete independence from the British rule.

Important Indo-Anglian novels reflecting the first phase of the Indian freedom movement are—*A Journal of Forty-eight Hours of the year* 1945 (1835) by K.C. Dutt and S.C. Dutt's three novels: *The Republic of Orissa: Annals from the Pages of the Twentieth Century* (1845), *The Young Zemindar* (1883), *Shunkur, A Tale of the Indian Mutiny of 1857* (1885), etc.

Novels reflecting the second phase of the Indian freedom struggle are—*The Prince of Destiny* (1909) by S.K. Ghose; *Hindupore* (1909) by S.M. Mitra, etc. and novels of the third phase of the Indian freedom struggle are—Sri Aurobindo's *New Lamps for Old* (1893-94); K.S. Venkataramani's *Murugan, the Tiller* (1927) and *Kandan, the Patriot* (1932); *Indira Devi* (1930) by A. Subrahmanya; *Untouchable* (1935) by M.R. Anand; *The Sword and the Sickle* (1942) by M.R. Anand; Shankar Ram's two volumes of short stories—*The Children of the Kaveri* (1927) and *Creatures All* (1931) and a novel—*Love of Dust* (1938); Raja Rao's *Kanthapura* (1938) and *The Cow of the Barricades* (1947); K. Nagarajan's *Athawar House* (1940—by Bombay Univ. 1939 by Iyengar and 1937 by Dorothy Spencer); R.K. Narayan's *Waiting for the Mahatma* (1955) and *Dodu and Other Stories* (n.d.); *Tomorrow Is Ours* (1943); and *Defeat for Death* (1944) both by K.A. Abbas; C.N. Zutchi's *Motherland* (1944); Aamir Ali's *Conflict* (1947); B. Bhattacharya's *So Many Hungers!* (1947), etc.

From a study of the struggle of the Indians for freedom from the colonial rule, we can define nationalism as a weapon for a dominated community to fight against the foreign rule of an imperialist country.

Nationalism may be interpreted, in the Indian context, as the efforts to consolidate the nation after Independence.

K.R. Minogue remarks: "This third phase of nationalism takes different forms like claiming additional territory, settling disputes over territory, efforts towards maintaining and tightening the homogeneity or integration of the nation, and striving for economic and cultural development."[14] All these and many other problems facing the nation after independence have been reflected in the novels and short stories published after independence. And some important historical novels are—Vimla Raina's *Ambapali* (1962); G.D. Khosla's *The Last Mughal* (n.d.); Manohar Malgonkar's *The Devil's Wind* (1972); Bhagwan S. Gidwani's *The Sword of Tipu Sultan* (1976), etc.

Of the political novels reflecting the freedom struggle with a sense of nostalgia or reminiscence mention may be made of the following: M.R. Anand's *Seven Summers* (1951); *Morning Face* (1968) and *Confession of a Lover* (1976); R.K. Narayan's *Waiting for the Mahatma* (1955); K.A. Abbas's *Inquilab* (1955); K. Nagarajan's *Chronicles of Kedaram* (1961); Venu Chitale's *In Transit* (1950); Zeenuth Futehally's *Zohra* (1951); S. Menon Marath's *Wounds of Spring* (1961) and *The Sale of an Island* (1968); Lambert Mascarenhas's *Sorrowing Lies My Land* (1955), etc.

Among the post-independence political novels reflecting the phenomenon of our attainment of freedom in a spirit of analytical reconstruction the important ones are—Kamala Markandaya's *Some Inner Fury* (1955); Khushwant Singh's *Train to Pakistan* (1956) and *I Shall not Hear the Nightingale* (1959); Attia Hosain's *Suinlight On a Broken Column* (1961) and short stories, *Phoenix Fled and Other Stories* (1953); Manohar Malgonkar's *Combat of Shadows* (1962) and *A Bend in the Ganges* (1964); Raj Gill's *The Rape* (1974); Mulk Raj Anand's *The Private Life of an Indian Prince* (1953); *Death of a Hero* (1963); *The Princes* (1963); Manohar Malgonkar's *Distant Drum* (1960); Bhabani Bhattacharya's *Shadow from Ladakh* (1966); Nayantara Sahgal's *A Time to be Happy* (1957), *This Time of Morning* (1965), *Storm in Chandigarh* (1969) and *The Day in Shadow* (1971); Arun

Joshi's *The Apprentice* (1974) and short stories, *The Survivor* (1975).

But the post-Independence era has produced many commercial novels without a concern for national or social issues like—Huthi Singh's *Maura* (1951); P.M. Nityanandan's *The Long, Long Days* (1960); Jyotshna Bhattacharjee's *Shadows in the Sunshine* (1965); Maya Balse's *The Sensuous Saint* (1975) or *Just a Matter of Mistresses* (1972) and Veena Nagpal's *Compulsion* (1975) and other novels.

Of the Spy thrillers—Manohar Malgonkar's *Spy in Amber* (1971) and *Beware Bombay* (1975); Aamir Ali's *Assignment in Kashmir* (1973) and Ruskin Bond's *An Axe for the Rani* (1972) are the popular ones.

Among the many sex-thrillers important ones are—Sasthi Brata's *Confessions of an Indian Woman Eater* (1971); Bunny Reuben's *You, I and Her* (1973); Nergis Dalal's *The Inner Door* (1975); Romen Basu's *A Gift of Love* (1976). But emphasising the importance of this category of novel Murli Das Melwani writes: "Its value to Indian society is the same as any other form of escaping entertainment; it lightens the burden of hard existence"[15]

Some of the post-independence social novels with a serious purpose where the novelists have portrayed the various causes of unhappiness of the people to find a society free of all ills are Mulk Raj Anand's *The Old Woman and the Cow* (1960) and *The Road* (1961); R.K. Narayan's *Mr. Sampath* (1949); *The Financial Expert* (1952); *The Guide* (1958); *The Man-Eater of Malgudi* (1962); *The Vendor of Sweets* (1967); *The Painter of Signs* (1976); and Stories, *A Horse and Two Goats* (1970); Raja Rao's *The Serpent and the Rope* (1960); *The Cat and Shakespeare* (1965) and *Comrade Kirillov* (1976); B. Bhattacharya's *Music for Mohini* (1952); *He Who Rides a Tiger* (1954) and *A Goddess Named Gold* (1960); G.V. Desani's *All About H. Hatterr* (1948); Sudhin N. Ghose's *And Gazelles Leaping* (1949); *Cradle of the Clouds* (1951); *The Vermilion Boat* (1953) and *The Flame of the Forest*

(1955); Kamala Markandaya's *Nectar in a Sieve* (1954); *Two Virgins* (1973); *The Coffer Dams* (1969), *A Handful of Rice* (1966); *A Silence of Desire* (1960) and *Possession* (1963); Ruth Prawer Jhabvala's *To Whom She Will* (1955); *Nature of Passion* (1956); *Esmond in India* (1958); *Get Ready for Battle* (1962); *The Householder* (1960); *A New Dominion* (1972); short stories *Like Birds, Like Fishes* (1963); *A Stronger Climate* (1968) and *An Experience of India* (1972); B. Rajan's *The Dark Dancer* (1959) and *Too Long in the West* (1961); Padmini Sengupta's *Red Hibiscus* (1962); Anita Desai's *Cry, the Peacock* (1963); *Voices in the City* (1965); *Bye-Bye, Black Bird* (1971) and *Where Shall We Go This Summer* (1975); Arun Joshi's *The Foreigner* (1968) and the *Strange Case of Billy Biswas* (1971); Dilip Hiro's *A Triangular View* (1969); *Saros Cowasjee's Goodbye to Elsa* (1975); Murli Das Melwani's stories—*Stories of a Salesman* (1967); Hamdi Bey's *Small Town Stories* (1974); Padma Hejmadi's *Coigns of Vantage* (1972); Timeri Murari's *The Marriage* (1973); Jai Nimbkar's *Temporary Answers* (1974); John B. Alphonso Karakala's *Passions of the Nightless Night* (1974), etc.

Thus, we have seen that nationalism in one aspect or the other, has been dealt with in many of the political and social novels of both the pre-independence and post-independence eras in Indo-Anglian literature. Quite aloof from these and other novels, Tagore's novels dealing with nationalism are discussed in details in Chapter 4 of this book.

REFERENCES

1. W.T. Stace, *A Critical History of Greek Philosophy* (London, 1962), 123.
2. Herschell Baker, *The Image of Man* (New York, 1961), 63.
3. *Ibid.*, 104.
4. H.O. Taylor, *The Humanism of Italy* (New York, 1962), 25.
5. Corliss Lamont, *Humanism as a Philosophy* (New York, 1950), 21f.
6. V.S. Naravane, *Modern Indian Thought* (Bombay, 1964), 113.
7. Mulk Raj Anand, *Apology for Heroism* (Bombay, 1957), 78.

8. K.R. Minogue, *Nationalism* (London, Methuen, 1969), Chapter IV.
9. Rabindranath Tagore, *Nationalism* (London, Macmillan, 1950), Chap. I
10. Hans Kohn, *Nationalism: Its Meaning and History* (New York, D. Van Nostrand & Co., 1965), 29.
11. K.R. Minogue, *Nationalism* (London, Methuen, 1969), 25.
12. G.P. Sarma, *Nationalism in Indo-Anglian Fiction* (New Delhi, Sterling Publishers Pvt. Ltd., 1978), 60.
13. K.R. Minogue, *Nationalism* (London, Methuen, 1969), 154.
14. *Ibid.*, 28-31.
15. Murli Das Melwani, "In Defence of Pulp Literature" in *Quest*, 100th No., March/April, 1976.

3

Tagore's English Novels: Critical Appraisal in Humanist Perspectives

(I) *BINODINI*

Rabindranath Tagore's first major novel, *Binodini* has attracted much attention from critics like George Sampson, Bhabani Bhattacharya, Niharranjan Ray, Humayun Kabir, V.S. Naravane, Masti Venkatesa Iyengar, Krishna Kripalani, R.C. Majumdar, Bimanbehari Majumdar, etc. for a variety of reasons. It has been hailed as "the first modern novel by an Indian author,"[1] "the beginning of a new pathway,"[2] "the first all-round psychological novel devoted to the study of social problems,"[3] and "one of the first and finest studies of woman's psychology in Bengali or indeed any other language."[4] Its distinction lies not only in its pioneering use of psychological realism in portraying characters, but also in its examination of the plight of young widows in Hindu Society through the larger perspective of their self-actualisation. In the exploration of the so-called redemptive choices which the Hindu ethos seem to offer to widows, Tagore "emerges as a non-conformist, ready to expose social conservatism."[5] The novel carries Tagore's suggestion that the amelioration of the lot of widows, *i.e.*, dispossession, depersonalisation and dehumanisation, does not lie merely in remarriage but also in creating conditions for the harmonious realisation of their personality or self-hood. Binodini's character is portrayed as possessing an extraordinary will of rejecting remarriage as a possible solution to her predicament. Rather than consenting to a socially unacceptable marriage, she seeks, through the dynamics of self-affirmation, a more meaningful role of her rich personality, acquiring thus "a grandeur even in her defeat."[6]

An evaluation of the novel will show the transition from Binodini's initial acceptance of traditional norms enjoined upon the Hindu widow to her revolt against them and her final self-abnegation. For the abundance of dialogue in the novel, Masti Venkatesa Iyengar remarked that it is "more like a play than like a novel"[7] Krishna Kripalani is of the opinion that with this novel Tagore has "laid out the foundation of the modern novel in Indian literature"[8] R.C. Majumdar remarks: "Rabindranath relied upon the detailed psychological method in which incidents and intentions are marshalled in a close array and every step in the evolution of the story and character is subjected to a process of a minute analysis."[9] It is a novel in which the author "watched the human drama with such a gentle and calm irony, without the intrusion of poetic rhapsodies or intellectual dissertations."[10] This is the first novel in Bengali in which "plot depends on character and not *vice versa*."[11]

The theme of the novel, the problems of the young Hindu widow and the humiliation she is subjected to by the society, had been used as a motif by Tagore's predecessor Bankim Chandra Chatterjee in his novels *Bisbriksha* (1873) and *Krishnakanter Vil* (1878). But unlike Bankim's heroines Kundanandini (in *Bisbriksha*) and Rohini (in *Krishnakanter Vil*) the character of Binodini is portrayed by Tagore with the dialectal tension and conflict of the feminine psyche: the anger, frustration and revenge natural to a charming and beautiful young widow, along with her great potentialities for deep compassion and self-sacrifice. K.R. Srinivasa Iyengar comments:

> Tagore's is a subtler, more convincing psychological study than either of the two novels of Bankim which exploit a similar theme.[12]

The most important feature in the novel is the human concern that Tagore reveals for the ordeal of consciousness of the young widow. Because he dared to depict her yearnings, frustrations and sufferings with sympathy and solicitude and thus succeeded in elevating the small story to epic heights.

The story of the novel is very simple and it centres round the problem of human relationship. A critical analysis of the main character Binodini's crisis and the denouement as an archetypal image of the tragic plight of a young Hindu widow will show Tagore's humanism. His humanism consists of his love for mankind and his emphasis on "man's role for emancipation of himself through emancipation of the whole of mankind."[13] There are six characters in the novel and of whom four are women characters. Among the four, "Binodini is the most real, convincing and full-blooded."[14] The development of the plot is related to her frustrations and suffering in which is summed up the author's ironic acceptance of the orthodox Hindu society of the day.

The narrative starts with a sidelight on the social conditions pertaining to marriage and family relationship. Binodini is the only child of her parents. Though she is beautiful, accomplished and tutored by an English governess, her marriage has become a problem for her mother as her father died without leaving enough money for her dowry. Her hand is offered to Mahendra, the son of the wealthy Rajlakshmi, an old friend of her mother's, who, after initial acceptance, backs out due to his aversion for an arranged marriage and the fear of the new bride's ousting his mother. Rajlakshmi could help her friend only by getting Binodini married to a distant cousin of hers "whose only claim to distinction was his excessively enlarged liver."[15] So she is soon widowed and condemned in full-blooded youth to a life of privation, denial and misery in a remote village. Three years later, on an impulse and against the wishes of his mother, the wayward Mahendra marries the unschooled, plain looking Asha, the niece of his aunt Annapurna. The bride is brought up by her uncle.

Very soon an estrangement develops between the possessive

mother and the wife-infatuated son. Rajlakshmi, unable to bear the sight of her son's uxoriousness goes away to her native village, accompanied by Bihari, Mahendra's close friend. There she is looked after with devotion and hospitality by Binodini and is very pleased by her treatment. At this stage, Binodini's image is free of psychological conflicts and complexities but we do get a glimpse of the simmering passions within her from the romantic thrill she experiences on reading Mahendra's letter to his friend, Bihari about his connubial joys. Her imagination, fed by the reading of romantic novels, is set aflame by her conjectures about the nature and form of physical love. Rajlakshmi sympathises her pitiful plight of loneliness. She is so charmed by Binodini's accomplishments that she brings her along with her to Calcutta when she returns home. Now the stage is set for a tempestuous drama of human emotions.

Binodini, with her beauty, grace, dignity and intelligence, wins the admiration of all including the "high-souled Bihari. The simple-minded Asha too is "overawed by her beauty and grace and the piercing intelligence of her eyes."[16] The more Asha sees Binodini, the more she feels inferior to her. Binodini's art of looking, demeanour, and speech easily charms the old fashioned Rajlakshmi. She regrets not making Binodini her daughter-in-law and tells her about it. Regretting his declining of the offer to marry Binodini Bihari says:

> I admit I was wrong. And yet it is better to lose by not marrying than to lose by marrying wrongly.[17]

Binodini commands admiration for the ease and spontaneity of her movements and alertness in attending to the needs of the inmates of the house. When Bihari and Rajlakshmi are Binodini's guests in her village, he is surprised to find his room "neatly and tidily arranged, fresh flowers and leaves in a brass vase."[18] Similarly, Mahendra too admires her skill in household duties which he notices when Asha is away at Kashi. One day he is surprised, on entering his room, to find the scene where "the mosquito net had a frill of pink silk which hung over a spotlessly white bed cover. The old-fashioned bolster had been replaced by square-cut cushion...."[19] When Binodini has taken charge of Mahendra's house, everything is well regulated and "the previous disorder and shabbiness were replaced by neatness and order."[20]

Binodini is also an embodiment of tender love and sympathy for other fellow beings. These feelings of love and sympathy represent Tagore's humanism. In the beginning of the story she is not jealous of Asha and loves her as a true friend and helps her in domestic works. She expresses deep concern for Asha to Bihari when she (Binodini) thinks of leaving Mahendra's house. She has great regard for Bihari. She is deeply hurt when Mahendra unjustly accuses Bihari as being secretly in love with Asha. Moved by this allegation she consoles Bihari like a mother who

> ...rocks the sick child in her arms, so Binodini rocked the unhappy image in her heart.[21]

Binodini has love and respect for Rajlakshmi. She joins Mahendra and Asha in their revelry, only after attending to the sick Rajlakshmi and discharging the household chores. She nurses the servants also when they are sick, with sympathy and care.

She has the capacity to study the psychology and minds of the people around her. In the beginning of the story she makes a fair assessment of Bihari, that he is all set to ruin her game and prepares to meet his challenge. She also suspects that Bihari is secretly in love with Asha. She also correctly assesses Rajlakshmi that she is responsible for her son's moral ruin and accuses her thus:

> Didn't you ever, out of spite against your daughter-in-law, wish this seductress to divert your son's mind? Look within yourself and see if it is not so![22]

She also makes a correct estimate of Mahendra's character and realises his infidelity and meanness. She is definite that

Mahendra has "neither the guts to love nor the guts to do your (his) duty!"[23]

Such general qualities of Binodini as well as the various stages of her love entanglement have to be studied closely to explore her character for investigation of Tagore's humanism in the novel.

The entry of Binodini into the life of Mahendra has set the love triangle, to which Bihari adds the fourth dimension. Her arrival marks the beginning of disaster in the lives of Mahendra, Asha, and Bihari.

The first stage of love entanglement of Binodini with Mahendra begins with her reading Mahendra's letter to Bihari. The letter creates curiosity in her mind about Mahendra and Asha and "the nature and form of their love." Making herself a close friend to Asha, Binodini satisfies her yearning for conjugal love by listening to Asha's narratives of her marital bliss. Their intimacy is so advanced that Asha addressed Binodini by the pet name "Eye Sore."

Very soon this stage of curiosity is followed by jealousy in the mind of Binodini, who feels that she has been cheated of all the good things in life by that "slip of a girl," Asha. Conscious of her superiority to the inept Asha in beauty, intelligence and skill in household affairs, and recalling how her hand was offered to Mahendra earlier, she bursts out in jealousy and resentment:

> This happiness, this passionate ardour of the husband was my due and should have been mine..... I could have ruled this house like a queen, could have made the husband into a slave and transformed both the household and the husband into something wonderful from the present shabby, silly state. What I was denied and deprived of now belongs to the slip of a girl, this little play-doll![24]

Binodini's grievance against Mahendra is further intensified by his pretended inattention to her:

> ....Why this indifference? As though she was a piece of furniture!
>
> Wasn't she human, wasn't she a woman ? If only he came to know her he would see the vast difference between her and his pet Chuni.[25]

Binodini resolves to avenge her humiliation by ensnaring Mahendra. At this point she has no deliberate plan to wreck the married life of Asha and Mahendra. Her such-thought reflects Tagore's humanism based on reason and philanthrophic nature and self-sacrifice. Her thought pattern is expressed thus:

> The nature of her own feelings towards Mahendra was not clear to her. She had not forgotten that he had spurned her hand in marriage and deprived her of her right to love and happiness.... Did she hate him for it and sought to avenge her wrong, or did she love him and wanted to offer herself in self-surrender? All she knew was that she was being consumed by a passionate flame inside her, whether of hate or of love or of both, she could not say. ....Do I wish to die or to destroy? Am I the hunter or the hunted? I wish I knew.[26]

The picture of Binodini at this stage of characterisation, as Srikumar Banerjee observes, "is that of a woman denied her right to love afire with jealousy, bent upon bringing Mahendra to his knees by all means, an archplotter, torn with mental conflict and repression."[27] But Tagore brings in Binodini's character a kind of steadying power which keeps in check any *femme fatale* streak in her. The love-crazy Mahendra precipitates a crisis by sneaking into her room at night and this leads to a rupture in her relationship with Rajlakshmi who accuses her of being a seductress. That she is not one is established beyond doubt by her letter of admonition to Mahendra:

> I have no right to love or be loved in this world. That is why I play at love to lighten my sorrow. .....I have no desire to play the game any longer.[28]

In her bid to satisfy her emotional urges, she has created a storm from which she sees no escape, except that which could be afforded by Bihari.

> Her desperate need of love as well as of protection drew her towards Bihari who seemed her only refuge. ....The shoulder that a woman can lean on must be strong, reliable and firm. Such a shoulder was Bihari's.[29]

So the see-saw of the conflicting sentiments and emotions of Binodini clearly prove that she is not a heartless and scheming seductress. "Her attitude is one of tempting him while retaining her own self-control."[30]

The second stage in the evolution of Binodini's character starts when a rift occurs between Bihari and Mahendra. Early in the story they take measure of each other. Bihari realises that "Binodini was not a girl to be either trifled with or ignored."[31] Similarly, Binodini also understands that Bihari is not a person to be fooled easily.

Once Bihari tells Binodini, in the very presence of Mahendra, that he (Mahendra) was "petted and spoilt by his mother and by his friends," and Asha is continuing the process. He advises Binodini, "turn your attention elsewhere instead of aiding and abetting his downfall."[32] Similarly, he warns Mahendra, saying, "Binodini is deliberately trying to seduce you and you, like a fool, are playing into her hands."[33]

But Bihari's impression that Binodini is a seductress undergoes a transition subsequently. The picnic to Dum-Dum garden helps Bihari to learn about Binodini's past. He realises for the first time that "Binodini looks a gay butterfly but deep inside her burns the austere light of a pure and devoted woman."[34] He feels that she looks an altogether different person.

The growing sympathetic understanding between Bihari and Binodini makes Mahendra jealous. He plans to get rid of Bihari. He openly accuses Bihari that he is secretly in love with Asha. Now Binodini's eyes are opened to the baser side of

Mahendra's character and this increases her admiration for Bihari. Here Tagore's humanism is seen openly when an honest human heart understands another honest human heart.

The third stage of Binodini's love begins with the reversal of Bihari's opinion about Binodini and her increased admiration for him. During Asha's absence from Calcutta Binodini attends on Mahendra, on the request of Asha and Rajlakshmi. This provides an opportunity to Binodini to study the character of Mahendra more thoroughly. Her contempt and hatred for Mahendra is increased when Mahendra mockingly says that she might be reading a letter from Bihari keeping it in the novel, *Vishavriksha*. She retorts:

> A jest! At whose expense? Were you worthy of his friendship, I could forgive your jest. But you are too mean, you are incapable of friendship and yet you have the check to gibe![35]

Bihari's understanding of a clean devoted woman in Binodini and his image of hers is shattered when he sees Mahendra, clasping Binodini's feet in his room, where she was about to sweep out of the room in a fury. Bihari apologises to Mahendra for his visit to Kashi, not knowing Asha was there. Mahendra his pride wounded, once again insults Bihari. With this, the rift between them is complete.

But this very incident increases Binodini's regard and love for Bihari. And for this reason, the wound inflicted by Bihari when he flung her away, violently, in a gesture of contempt, appears very sacred to her. She does not allow Mahendra even to touch the wound and she does not apply anything to heal it. After this, her love for Bihari turns into devotion. So, when Mahendra professes love to Binodini, she says:

> "At one time you thought you were in love with Asha. It was false. Now you imagine you are in love with me. That too is false. You love only yourself,"[36] and makes no secret of her real feeling towards him by writing a letter; "Today out of pity for you I renounce you."[37]

In spite of Binodini's taunts, Mahendra pursues her with repeated declarations of love. She is compelled to tell Bihari:

> Mahendra is in love with me. ...I have come to you for protection."[38]

Now Bihari fails to understand the irksome position in which Binodini is placed. He feels that her behaviour is "melodramatic, theatrical" and asks her to return to her village. He denies her request for a kiss to keep as "a moment's memory, to cherish till my death."[39]

The fourth and last stage of her love consists of her penance for the fulfilment of her love for Bihari. Obeying Bihari's orders with devotion Binodini retires to her village where she finds life unbearable as she is branded a harlot and vilified. To escape from this unbearable condition she agrees to elope with Mahendra who follows her even to the village on the promise that he would not do anything against her wishes. She does not even allow him to go to the railway station with her in the carriage, but asks him to go on foot. Bimanbehari Majumdar remarks:

> It was a case of the strangest elopement in the world.[40]

She goes to Calcutta with him in order to find Bihari herself. She has but one goal—to vindicate herself before Bihari.

After a long struggle, Binodini is able to locate the villa in Allahabad where Bihari lived for a short time. Towards the end when Bihari comes to Allahabad in search of Mahendra to take him to attend on his ailing mother, he finds Binodini in a room in the villa bedecked with flowers. Bihari becomes very angry as he imagines her to have led an unclean life with Mahendra. But she dispels such doubts by proclaiming that she did not defile herself but

> "...remained chaste. Your image, hard and severe, ordering me into exile—this image I have carried in my heart, hard and severe like burnished gold, like a precious stone.... I touch your feet and swear that nothing has happened to destroy this value."[41]

Bihari believes every word she utters and offers to marry her. But Binodini, with a spirit of self-abnegation does not accept him:

> Then let these words be my final reward. I want nothing more than what you have just affirmed. If I took more it would not last. Religion and society would never tolerate it.[42]

Binodini's renunciation, coming as it does after the resolute manner in which she has sought Bihari's love and won it, has led to much critical comment. Bimanbihari Majumdar refuted the charge that want of courage prevented Tagore to allow Binodini to be married to Bihari. He pointed out that "Tagore in the story *Tyaga* (Renunciation) written as early as 1892 allowed the heroine, Kusum, a Kayastha widow to marry Hemanta, a Brahmin young man."[43] The same writer feels that had the novel ended in her (Binodini's) marriage with Bihari, it would have become melodramatic.

Indeed, Binodini is the most powerful character created by Tagore in his novels. Niharranjan Ray acclaims:

> She (Binodini) has lent colour and vitality to its story from one end to the other, her radiant youth is the life-blood of the whole novel.[44]

It may be said that Binodini heralds the emergence of a new class of emancipated Indian women, who are no longer prepared to be downtrodden by society but fight to assert their rights. Through Binodini, Tagore portrays the love of a young widow convincingly and with much sympathy. And here we see Tagore's humanism blossoming to the full form keeping human value and human problem at the core of discussion. Binodini's sacrifice invests her as "the symbol of the stricken conscience of the contemporary middle-class Hindu society."[45]

I conclude my study with Krishna Kripalani's remark that Tagore's protest against the contemporary society's prejudices against widows constitute "a lasting shame to the Hindu conscience."[46]

(II) *THE WRECK*

The Wreck, Rabindranath Tagore's second novel in English, may be viewed in the humanist perspective for many reasons. Love is the pervading theme in this novel and small incident like a boatwreck complicated the love story of the main characters, Ramesh and Hemnalini. But the love triangle ensues with the introduction of the character of Kamala. The major characters of this novel undergo a lot of suffering and mental agony for no fault of theirs, like the characters in the books of Thomas Hardy. The novelist has depicted the psychological doubts and conflicts of the characters with great skill and sympathy.

The novel is an enactment of the Hindu notion of the sacredness and inviolability of marital ties. It dramatises the social and emotional imbroglio that results from the accidental exchange of a bride, a situation not entirely unknown even in modern times as the bride and bridegroom, meeting as strangers for the first time, may fail for some reason or the other to identify each other immediately. Though the novel ends with the affirmation of marital sanctity—the inviolate bride restored to her true husband—it perceptively records the embarrassments, disappointments, and tensions that result from the Hindu society's rigid observance of the ideal.

This novel has received conflicting reviews from various critics. Some praise it highly while others condemn it as a novel of absurdities and inconsistencies. Some Western critics find it "incredibly bad." The American reviewers of *The Wreck* complain that "the complexities of Hindu character and behaviour left them too puzzled to value the work highly."[47] However, Professor Lesny considers it "one of Tagore's best novels...homogeneous... full of action, and the human interest is very powerful."[48] Of the Indian critics S.C. Sengupta is of the opinion that in *The Wreck* "although not free from defects, the plot is ingeniously conceived and carefully constructed."[49] On the other hand, critics like Niharranjan Ray regard it as "a frankly romantic novel of flabby structure and poor substance."[50] In the same strain B.C. Chakravorty feels that "the development of characters is neither logical nor realistic. There are many absurdities and inconsistencies in this book."[51] Masti Venkatesa Iyengar too joins in condemning the novel by saying that the foundation is weak and "its superstructure commonplace and one has not a feeling of much satisfaction in its art when laying it down."[52]

Srikumar Banerjee considers the situations in the novel as "somewhat strange and unbelievable," and, according to Sujit Mukherjee, the novel is "under handicap from the very beginning because the situation which makes the story possible is brought about through a highly calculated accident."[53] Since the novel is predominantly based on the play of chance and coincidence, it lacks in the principle of "probability." To the sophisticated reader of today, the incidents in the novel may seem implausible but it cannot be denied that the novel does have both sociological and psychological truth if viewed against the matrix of social and emotional life of its characters. Edward Thompson makes the perceptive comment that *The Wreck* "shows how the Hindu family relationships are based not on human feelings but on conventional respect and worship."[54] But in spite of these criticisms none can deny the novel's popularity which can be "gauged from the fact that with the exception of *Gitanjali*, no other book of Tagore has been translated into so many languages."[55] The novel has to be viewed not as a mere episodic romance but as a sensitive study of the complex problems and dilemmas which the central characters, Ramesh and Kamala, face after the wreck against the background of the Hindu ideal of marriage. And this sensitive study of the complex problems and dilemmas facing the central characters involves Tagore's humanism which places human problems and sympathy at the centre.

Regarding the presence of chance and coincidence in the novel, one has to accept the interplay of the inexplicable factors in human life. There can be a place for them in human life.

Ramesh's inability to extricate himself from the compulsive situation he is placed in and Kamala's failure to appreciate his exemplary conduct create an impression that they are fitted to a pattern of predetermined incidents as they do not appear to assert either their individuality or self-identity. This, in a sense, drains off the vitality in characters or even in the value system that the novel projects. Here the novelist shows sympathy for these characters and this sympathy carries the strong stamp of Tagore's humanism. So Humayun Kabir remarks that though the foundation of the novel is weak and full of accidents and coincidences yet the.... "characters are, by and large, solid and stand out as men and women of flesh and blood."[56]

The first mischance— the mistaking of Kamala for his bride— is brought about by Ramesh's own naivety and lack of resolution. Though deeply in love with Hemnalini, he has neither declared his love to her nor given a thought to any likely impediment for their marriage—he, being the son of an orthodox Hindu and her family being Brahmo Samajists. When his father fixes his marriage with a girl from a far-off village, he makes a feeble protest and hopes that "some accident might still prevent the marriage."[57] His protest against the marriage takes an absurd form:

> The wedding duly took place, but Ramesh refused to recite the sacred formula correctly, closed his eyes when the time arrived for the "auspicious look" (the privileged moment when bridegroom and bride see each other for the first time), wore a hang-dog expression, and kept his mouth shut during the jesting in the bridal chamber, lay throughout the night with his back turned to the girl, and left the room as early as possible in the morning (7-8).

A storm strikes the wedding party during their return journey by boat, killing all except Ramesh. On regaining consciousness, he looks around for his people and finds only a maiden in crimson dress, she, in fact, belonging to another wedding group, wrecked nearabouts. Mistaking her to be his bride, he takes her home. This mistaking of Kamala for his real bride Susila is the result of Ramesh's negligence of the ritual performance of the marriage. Had he not closed his eyes during the moments of the "auspicious look" he would easily recognise Kamala and not mistaken her as Susila. Srikumar Banerjee[58] and B.C. Chakravorty[59] have questioned why Ramesh takes three months to detect that the bride he has taken home is not really his. One plausible answer to such a question is that Ramesh's father and several of his kinsfolk had died in the disaster that overtook their boat and he was too preoccupied with settling their affairs to pay any attention to his bride; it would have been improper for him to pay attention to her soon after the tragedy. She was shunned by the village women and hence, there was no occasion to discover the truth about her. When after the lapse of three months, Ramesh is shocked to learn that her name is not Susila, his own bride, but Kamala.

> Ramesh's heart gave a throb of dismay and the colour left his face. The conviction was suddenly forced upon him that there had been a terrible mistake somewhere (17).

Though he knows the truth, in the prevailing social milieu, she cannot be sent back to her husband, even if he were alive and if he were to tell her the truth, she would not accept his protection.

> Ramesh now set himself to think out a future plan of action. Her husband had in all probability been drowned. Even if he could find out where the husband's people lived and send Kamala to them it was very doubtful if they would receive her; and it would not be fair to send her back to her uncle's house.... Even if her husband were alive was it likely that he would wish or dare to take her back? He could not keep her with him on any footing except that of a wife, and he could not hand her over to any one else; and yet, he and she could not live together as man and wife (19).

Hoping that he can discover a solution in the anonymity of

Calcutta, Ramesh takes her there and as a temporary solution puts her as a boarder in a girls' school, declaring her as his wife which is another example of his slow-witted miscalculation. Here we see Tagore's humanism blossoming in the form of Ramesh's sympathy and love for a fellow human girl Kamala.

Thrown back into Hemnalini's company in Calcutta, Ramesh becomes engaged to her and gives his consent to an immediate wedding. In his muddled way, he hopes to remove any misunderstanding by revealing all that happened to Hemnalini who, in turn, would explain to Kamala her true situation. Kamala would find a friend in Hemnalini and would readily agree, he hopes, to make her home with the young couple. Akshay Babu upsets his plan by prematurely revealing Kamala's existence to Hemnalini's family and also news is received that she is unwilling to stay in school and is coming back. He puts off the marriage by a weak hoping to resolve the muddle but the impracticability of his scheme is revealed when he is confronted with a demand for an explanation of his relationship with Kamala by Hemnalini's brother. Weak-willed, though noble-minded, Ramesh once again takes recourse to flight, this time a long voyage on the Ganges. On the steamer and later at Ghazipur in uncle Chakrabarti's house, Ramesh feels drawn to Kamala enchanted by her beauty and self-effacing solicitude for him. His pathetic attempts to reveal the truth to her in the form of a story and other indirect methods do not succeed and feeling unable to prolong the dilemma, he ponders:

> I don't see how I'm going to live with her and keep my distance. I can't keep it up any longer. After all, Kamala really is my wife (172).

But he cannot implement his decision because of his indecisiveness and his inability to erase Hemnalini's image from his mind. Urged to action by uncle Chakrabarti, he writes a farewell message to Hemnalini, giving a full account of the happenings, and unable to deliver the letter to her at Calcutta, returns with it to Ghazipur and with his "extraordinary carelessness" (202) leaves it about; a page of this falls into Kamala's hands and sets in motion the final denouement—a truly Hardyean situation.

At Ghazipur Kamala's sudden disappearance leads Ramesh to think that she has committed suicide. Having failed to resolve the tangle himself, he feels that this is the best way out, as he tells Hemnalini's brother later on:

> ....it was the only possible solution for her. The pair of us were in such a tangle that I shudder to think of the difficulties with which we should ultimately have been faced, had she not cut the Gordian Knot in this way (284).

After it Ramesh makes a brief appearance in Benares where he meets, to his amazement, Kamala as well as Hemnalini to whom he bares his heart in a confession:

> ...I can never forget the only two women who have ever found a place in my heart, and to cherish their memory all my life will be an inestimable boon to me (386).

Confronted by fate with a dilemma to which he does not find himself equal, Ramesh takes refuge in a kind of naive idealism allowing events to overtake him again and again. He cannot extricate himself from his suffering because of his weak-will, irresoluteness and lack of moral certitude.

Only after reading the unposted letter of Ramesh to Hemnalini Kamala realises her position *vis-a-vis* Ramesh. In the letter Ramesh makes a clean breast of his relations with Kamala. Thereafter, the main story is concerned with the efforts of Kamala to find her husband, Nalinaksha and later, her union with him. Hemnalini's marriage with Ramesh is completely relegated to the background. The plot is, thus, developed through a series of errors, accidents and is based on the "dilemma of mistaken identity, resulting in an exchanging of wives, delightfully told...."[60]

Kamala's attitudes, motivations, and behaviour are shaped by the cultural environment in which she has been brought up.

An orphaned village girl, her wedding is suddenly arranged by her miserly uncle to a complete stranger as no dowry is demanded. As she later recounts to Sailaja, she felt too shy to look at the groom during the marriage:

> You see, I was almost past the marrying age, then all of a sudden a marriage was arranged for me and the other girls teased me dreadfully. So just to show that I didn't consider myself extraordinarily lucky in getting a husband at my age, I never even glanced at him (348-49).

When she is rescued by Ramesh from the boat wreck, it is no wonder she takes him to be her husband. She is puzzled and pained by Ramesh's reservedness towards her but as a self-effacing Hindu wife, she subordinates her feelings and unquestioningly obeys his whims. Her delight in simple things and a certain pride of self save her from becoming utterly miserable. During their stay at uncle Chakrabarti's house at Ghazipur, she becomes fully conscious of the strange relationship between her and Ramesh as it is thrown into sharp contrast with the happy intimate married life of Sailaja, the uncle's daughter.

Kamala's reactions to the crucial revelation of the true state of affairs are significant. She comes to know from the letter that Ramesh had discovered that she was not his wife and was in fact in love with another woman but had been unable to resolve the entanglement that Fate had brought about. As an orthodox Hindu lady, she is shocked that she had calmly assumed him to be her husband and was preparing to settle with him:

> Shame pierced her heart like a dagger, and as various incidents recurred to her memory, she would gladly have sunk into the floor. Disgrace would cling to her all her life; there was no escape from its stigma (204).

As if to add insult to injury, she receives a letter of endearment from Ramesh who, now, appears to her as an ogre. She ought to be thankful, as Sailaja tells her later on, that she fell into Ramesh's hands and no one else's but at the moment, she feels only repulsion:

> ....If after their arrival in Ghazipur her heart had warmed towards him, did he imagine it was because he was Ramesh and not because he was as she believed—her husband (210-11).

Kamala now resolves to seek out her true husband whose name is revealed in the confession of Ramesh which has fallen accidentally in her hands:

> If I would be a true wife to him, I must live to prostrate myself at his feet. While life endures, he is not lost to me (311).

With the help of uncle Chakrabarti she is inducted into his house as Haridasi and is ultimately united with Nalinaksha. The sequence of events which traces the fortunes of Ramesh and Kamala is directed, it will be seen, towards an enactment of the sanctity of marriage which appears wrecked by the intervention of chance and accident but which triumphs in the end because of the steadfast commitment of Kamala to its ideal. The psychological issue that the novel poses is admirably summed up by M.M. Bhattacharjee:

> Can a Hindu wife who has never seen her husband and, under peculiar circumstances, has come to look upon another as such and adored him sincerely forswear her love and transfer it automatically to the former when she knows the truth? Is it likely that love and the conventional idea of fidelity to marriage ties will have equal weight with her, and the conflict will end in tragedy?[61]

It is explicit that at no time did Kamala fall in love with Ramesh. It is true that she did feel drawn to him and wondered about the restraint that he observed in his relations with her. But once she knows the truth, whatever tender feelings she has entertained towards him in the mistaken belief that he is her husband, evaporate and she is shocked and repelled by his letter, addressing her as "Dearest"—she considers it a "filthy thing."

> ...It was a proposal that she should make a house for a man who was not her husband. Fully cognizant of all the facts, Ramesh has bided his time to fling this insult at her (210).

Judged from her reaction, it is clear that her conduct is in no way illogical and the course of action she adopts follows logically from her ingrained faith in marital sanctity.

The restoration of Kamala to her husband, Nalinaksha, is rendered easy by his compassionate nature and a perspective on marriage which is free of the complications of romantic love. The prime object of his life is the happiness of his mother who was separated from her husband who had joined the Brahmo Samaj and married a widow. But Nalinaksha dissociated himself from Brahmo Samaj for the sake of this orthodox mother and is on the lookout for a bride who would fit in with his mother's rigid views on ceremonial purity. He tells his mother:

> ...I had always intended to give you a little surprise by bringing you an orthodox little Hindu daughter-in-law. I knew quite well that if I married a grown-up Brahmo lady none of us would be happy (305).

Nalinaksha comes across Kamala in one of his trips and marries her, only to lose her in the tempest that overturned his boat, the same that hit Ramesh's party. Unable to locate her after the storm, he gives her up as dead. Nearly a year later, he comes to know, through Ramesh's confession, her story. Kamala has been inducted meanwhile into his house as Haridasi and wins his mother's heart entirely. Nalinaksha himself is deeply impressed by her silent devotion to him and they are united, his brief engagement to Hemnalini proving no obstacle to their union. Thus Tagore's humanism prevails in his solution of the love entanglement by giving sympathetic consideration on the character of Kamala.

The character and experiences of Hemnalini go to serve the novelist's purpose of revealing "the prevailing distance between the Hindus and the Brahmos,"[62] and the emergence of a new type of womanhood under the influence of the progressive Brahmo Samaj and female education, just then coming into vogue. She exhibits a rare constancy of love and loyalty towards Ramesh but the latter's indecisiveness, lack of grit and inability to release himself from the grip of circumstances that overtake him render their love unfruitful. Though the mix-up of Ramesh and Kamala is successfully cleared at the end, no rapprochement is indicated between Ramesh and Hemnalini. Though outwardly tranquil throughout the story, the latter is riven with an inward sorrow.

> ...She wore an air of supreme melancholy and resignation that was like a permanent twilight on her features (408).

Though Tagore accomplishes the happy reunion of Kamala and Nalinaksha as a vindication of the Hindu marital sanctity, he pinpoints through the disappointed love of Ramesh and Hemnalini the sad consequences of the system of arranged marriages. The plot construction of *The Wreck* is not satisfactory to many critics as the plot is full of improbabilities. But they have admired its characterisation. Among the characters, Kamala is the most interesting, lively and full-blooded. As the heroine, she dominates the whole action with her natural charm, grace and modesty.

To sum up, *The Wreck* bears the stamp of Tagore's humanism in the portrayal of the character of Kamala who excels all the traditional heroines of Tagore like Asha, Sharmila and Niraja, by her qualities of humility, self-restraint and self-effacement. Tagore seems to believe that such women can bring the much needed stability to the restless domestic world dominated by men. Further, it "contributes to the growth of the Bengali novel by its concern with the contemporary society and its problems."[63] Commenting on the treatment of Humanism in the novel Dr. A.V. Krishna Rao gives a fitting remark:

> *The Wreck* is fanciful. It is a social fantasy. The play of fate or chance in human lives is fancifully depicted.[64]

(III) *CHATURANGA*

Various critics have interpreted *Chaturanga* more as a short story rather than a novel. Pulinbihari Sen and Subhendusekhar Mukhopadhyaya in their bibliography on Rabindranath Tagore's short stories and novels have grouped Chaturanga both under the category of novels and short stories. Dr. S.C. Sengupta hesitates whether "*Broken Ties* (*Chaturanga*) is a novel at all for it had not that completeness, that gradual building of plot on character we expect from a novel."[65] To Masti Venkatesa Iyengar *Chaturanga* is "really a short story." According to Humayun Kabir it is "a long story rather than a novel."[66] Similarly, K.R. Srinivasa Iyengar too listed it in Tagore's short stories. However, Ashok Mitra, the English translator of *Chaturanga* called it a "novella"[67] in his translator's note.

This novel *Chaturanga* may be viewed in the humanist perspective with humanism as the theme. Human feelings, rather than events, become the main material of this novel. It is hailed as a " work of art without blemish." It is a great novel with a compact and wellknit plot embedded with music and poetry. Famous critic Niharranjan Ray says that *Chaturanga* "is an exquisite and unforgettable work of art."[68] S.C. Sengupta remarks that "it rivals the English *Gitanjali* and Bengali *Balaka*."[69] Similarly, Krishna Kripalani proclaims this short novel as "one of Tagore's best."[70] Humayun Kabir too comments that "*Chaturanga* has been regarded by many as one of the best examples of Tagore's craftsmanship."[71] In *Chaturanga* Tagore devises intellectual discussions and convincing situations for asserting the importance of man above all pseudo-religious traditions and narrow-minded sectarianism and nationalism. He protests against all kinds of barriers of the family, the caste, the rituals, the sects, the groups, the party, the nation, the administration, etc. that divide men and dwarf their personalities.

Chaturanga stands out as Tagore's most interesting experiment in the novel form inasmuch as he tries to achieve in it a pattern of thought and feeling, symphonic in structure and syncretistic in import. The underlying musical form helps him in the orchestration of ideas, ideologies and emotions, and, as pointed out by Ashok Mitra, "gives the strangely agitated stormy world of *Chaturanga* its still point."[72] Here Tagore achieves a fusion of the poet and the novelist, for it depends more on theme and mood than on the plot. Tagore's art underwent a significant change after the publication of his epic novel, *Gora.* His tour of Europe might have stimulated him to use the new techniques of the novel, in vogue on the continent, especially in France. Humayun Kabir feels that the French influence on Tagore is seen in that he "moved towards the dominance of theme over plot and simultaneously of the mind over the heart."[73]

In *Chaturanga,* Tagore exposes the religious fanatics who, in the name of Hindu orthodoxy and Vaishnavism, indulge in religious aberrations and self-exhibitionism and mislead the people from the true path of spirituality. Here the conflict is between *love and religion, rather spiritual versus sensual.* The novel portrays the dialectical relation between the spiritual and the secular in man's quest for self-realisation. The confrontation and conflict between the two is sought to be projected through the career of Sachis whose predicament becomes more complicated by his being subject to the pulls of the sensual in the form of Damini. "The intellectual and emotional dilemmas of Sachis are presented against the cross-currents of religious and reformative movements that rocked the Hindu society in Bengal in the second half of the nineteenth century."[74] In this novel Sribilas, the friend of the protagonist, narrates the whole story. Elements of humanism abound in this novel as the novelist dives deep into the inner labyrinths of the human mind and analyses their criss-cross psychological conflicts.

Among the four principal characters, Jagmohan, Sachis, Damini and Sribilas, identified in that order with the four parts—the Chaturanga of the novel—Sachis alone manifests an intense concern with the self, a concern which leads to a dissociation from wordly bonds and a search for the meaning of life within himself. It is in relation to him that the other characters in the novel need to be analysed and assessed so that their role in his spiritual growth and fulfilment can be appreciated.

The protagonist Sachis has been nurtured in the rationalist-atheist-humanist creed of his uncle Jagmohan whose career resembles in many respects that of the well-known radicals of the nineteenth century Bengal like Iswar Chandra Vidyasagar and David Hare. A wave of atheism swept over the student community of Calcutta and a fierce controversy raged between the die-hard Hindu bigots and those who professed sceptical rationalism imbibed through Western education. Jagmohan, who evidently belongs to this generation, has made it his life mission to blast theism but his assertions do not remain merely nihilistic; they assume the positive form of service to mankind in a true altruistic spirit without expectation of reward or fame. Under the tutelage of his uncle, Sachis not only acquires a mastery of English language but also imbibes, in full measure, Bentham's philosophy of "the greatest good of the greatest number," Mill's agnosticism and Comte's 'positivist' creed of *vivre pour autrue* (to live for one's neighbour).

Sachis co-operated Jagmohan, his adoptive uncle, in his efforts at the upliftment of his Muslim and Chamar neighbours. This brings Jagmohan into conflict with his neighbour and younger brother Harimohan—Sachis's father—whose religious orthodoxy is as strident as his brother's atheism. Jagmohan loses his share of income from the family property—a religious trust—but carries on his humanitarian work undaunted. He gives shelter, despite the protest and threats of his family, to Nanibala, a young pregnant widow who had been seduced and thrown out by Sachi's brother Purandhar. Sachis offers to marry her, thus proving himself a true disciple of his uncle. But, she commits suicide as she cannot forget her seducer and is ashamed to marry someone else. Here Tagore's humanism is seen in

Sachis's sympathy and love for other fellow-beings. Soon the city is devastated by plague and Jagmohan himself dies while serving the plague victims, having converted his house into a private hospital for the low caste Chamars and Muslims—his final affirmation of his ideals. Thus the first phase of Sachis's career with his uncle provides him a postulate of rationalism and dedicated service to man as a possible course for the realisation of self-fulfilment in life. This dedicated service to man is an aspect of Tagore's humanism which emphasises the well-being of all man.

Sachis is overwhelmed by the death of his uncle who had been to him "both father and friend—one may even add, son as well" (37). Unable to bear the void, he wanders from place to place and becomes the ardent disciple of Leelananda Swami—a self-proclaimed Vaishnava guru. Under the intoxication of religious devotion, Sachis indulges himself in frenzied "Kirtan" singing, massaging of the Guru's feet and becoming completely oblivious of the world outside till an assault in the shape of the irrepressible, self-willed and dominant Damini is launched on his spiritual absorption. Commenting on this phase of Sachis's career, Krishna Kripalani writes:

> Vaishnavism is a religion which seeks to realise God by a life of emotional self-abandon. Tagore who loved the poetry it inspired had a wholesome contempt for emotional self-exhibitionism into which in practice it had degenerated and found in the novel an excellent opportunity to show how religious emotion divorced from humanism is little better than a form of self-hypnosis or an opiate.[75]

Tagore's treatment of the Sachis-Damini relationship which forms the central theme of the novel seems to be an attempt at delineating the intricate issue of the spiritual versus the sensual. Lilananda Swami establishes his camp along with his prize—disciples, Sachis and Sribilas, in Calcutta in the house of Damini, whose name signifies "the lightening in the heart of the Sravana rain clouds, heaving with youthfulness to outward view but flickering with restless fires within" (45). A young widow, she has been consigned to the care of the Guruji, *i.e.*, Lilananda Swami, along with all her property by her late husband. To Sachis, who is so absorbed in his religious ecstasies that he is not even aware of such a place as Calcutta, her acts of defiance of the Guruji prove highly disturbing. Entering his room one day at an unaccustomed hour, he finds Damini prone on the ground, knocking her head on it and muttering, "Stone, O you Stone, have pity on me, have pity, kill me" (49).

Some time later, stranded in a cave for the night along with other disciples, Sachis has the harrowing experience of an attempt at seduction by Damini. He records the scene in his diary in moving imagery:

> ...then something which I imagined to be a wild beast grabbed my feet. But a wild beast has fur, this had none...it was horrible precisely because it was so soft and clammy, that heap of hunger.... Its breath was heavy and fast, I did not know what the face was like. I kicked and kicked throwing my legs about (52).

Sachis, who believes that human love is a trap, tries to avoid her but cannot help being aware of her. He persuades her to leave the place as she is not a believer in the guru. She refuses to go away on the plea that she has no other shelter. Now Sachis begs Damini's forgiveness for asking her to go away and requests her to join them in devotional music and discourse. This marks a turning point in Daminis's attitude; realising to what rigorous tests she has subjected Sachis, she overcomes her passion, and touching his feet in obeisance promises him "I *shan't* ever transgress" (70).

Sachis's faith in the Guruji has been faltering for some time. He starts as a formidable atheist and then plunges into religious intoxication which he abandons to retire into self-meditation. His quest for God-realisation now leads him to renounce all human bonds and take to solitary contemplation. After several days of intense meditation, Sachis believes that he has seen the light at last and expounds a philosophy of progress through contradiction: God shedding this freedom to assume Form and Man impatient to transcend his bondage in his yearning for the Formless. To quote Sachis, "...you limit yourself in me while I try to seek the limitless in you" (88). Though Damini does not understand the metaphysics of this she is ever grateful to Sachis for having rescued her from the fires of passion which would otherwise have consumed her. She is now devoted to his welfare but her attempts to protect him in the storm, are misconstrued by Sachis who begs her:

> I desperately need Him whom I am seeking; I have need for nothing else. Have pity on me, Damini, leave me alone (90).

Damini requests Sribilas to take her to Calcutta where they later get married. They move into the house which uncle Jagmohan had bequeathed to Sachis and revive the social work for the Muslim and Chamar neighbours. Sachis comes to Calcutta on a brief visit to give away Damini as a bride and when Sribilas request him to join their work, he replies, "No, I am afraid, my work lies elsewhere" (97). Here we see even other characters than the protagonist are characterised with sympathy for the downtrodden people and thought for their social welfare.

It is also seen that Sachis's shifting postures are perplexing. The motivation for such shifting is not adequately depicted. The divine frenzy under Lilananda Swami runs counter to all that he imbibed from his uncle earlier. His explanation that his uncle gave him the freedom of choice is understandable but his sudden ofting for a religious life is intriguing. His quitting the fold of Lilananda Swami can be understood, but the light towards which he ultimately finds himself advancing remains undiscernible to the reader. Here it is worth quoting Srikumar Banerjee's remark: "It is extremely difficult to discover any psychological norm in Sachis's wayward dilettantism and sudden spurts of eccentric behaviour."[76]

Tagore seems to symbolise in Sachis the divine yearning of a Ramakrishna or Vivekananda towards a mystic union with God. Sachis does not attend the kind of transcendence which these saints had. What his experience exemplifies is a quest towards it by an active consciousness subject to the pulls and counterpulls respectively of the spiritual and the sensual.

Damini, like Binodini of the earlier novel, employs many stratagems to win the heart of her lover and the cave scene where she attempts a seduction has a parallel with Binodini's attempt to win over Bihari in his room at night. Both are saved from possible surrender to passion by the nobility and strength of the men they love.

Damini, with her woman's instinct, understands Sachis, who considers love only as an evil snare standing between him and his spiritual quest. She renounces her love for him and accepts him as her spiritual guide. Despite her unflinching devotion to Sachis, she is able to marry Sribilas, the friend of Sachis, in strange circumstances. She helps him in his humanitarian work. After one year of marriage Damini dies, due to pain in her heart. She exhibits a rare capacity to self-abnegation which enables Sachis to pursue his path towards spiritual sublimation. This philanthropic work of Sribilas and Damini's self-abnegation represent another aspect of Tagore's humanism. But Sribilas's new humanism is theistic and is connected not only with head but also with heart.

Tagore has delineated the character of Damini as a vivacious young woman who attracts everyone with her grace and glitter, as her name suggests. She is "so real that no reader having known her can ever forget her."[77] Likewise, Masti Venkatesa Iyengar also remarks that "she interests us so deeply because she is extraordinary."[78] All the major characters, besides Damini, are also portrayed as fragments, though individualised. They are seen as part of the total personality of Sachis and his quest. They are less important before the chief protagonist and what interests us mainly in the book is the spiritual rather than the narrative content that is important.[79]

The novel is remarkable for its innovative narrative technique and its fusion of lyrical poetry with its content. The story is told from the point of view of Sribilas, one of the central characters. He narrates the story as a participant and witness to the events. He is full of admiration and sympathy for the protagonist. This admiration and sympathy represents an aspect of Tagore's humanism. In the execution of the plot and in delineating the wonderful, psychological analysis of characters, it is a work of exceptional value. Dr. S.C. Sengupta observes as: "There is something ethereal about the story and something elfin about the characters."[80]

Chaturanga is essentially a philosophic novel wherein Sachis's struggle to save himself from all forms of physical, intellectual and emotional attachments that lead to bondage are dramatised. In the pattern of the traditional pathways of spiritual redemption, Sachis experiments with salvation through works, *i.e.*, "Karma Yoga." He experiences an emotional crisis with the demise of his uncle which indicates that he has not attained perfect peace and happiness. Giving up the service principle, he takes shelter in "Bhakti Yoga" with Lilananda Swami. He is, however, not satisfied with the spells of emotional euphoria, threatened by Damini's intervention. A man of single-minded dedication, he yearns to control his desires and passions and takes to self-mortification to gain knowledge of self. This stage of "Jnana Yoga" takes him away from the world of senses and gives him inner strength to resist the temptations represented by Damini. Sachis is still wary of Damini and moves towards "Dhyana Yoga", the final important step towards spiritual enlightenment and devotes himself wholly to meditation in seclusion. His final bid is to conquer the ego for gaining freedom.

Sachis appears to be incapable of making any explicit statements concerning his religious experience and seems to be lost in the labyrinths of spirituality. His predicament is, however, a complex one in that he is subject to conflicting influences exemplified by Jagmohan, Lilananda Swami, and Damini. The complexities of his experience are aptly indicated by the title of the novel which also means Chess.

To sum up, *Chaturanga* is a small novel of only four characters and four chapters. But it is "one of the finest, one of the tensest and one of the most compact and competent works of art that Tagore ever produced."[81] The character of Damini is sharply individualised. She is the symbol of the social change and advancement of women that had started taking place in the early decades of this century. Since Tagore has made human feelings the main material of the novel, it is really a novel based on humanism. His humanism was born of his belief in spiritualism. He is a staunch humanist because he is a profound spiritualist.

(IV) *FAREWELL, MY FRIEND*

Farewell, My Friend is a novel based on Tagore's humanism which is visible in his awareness of life and problems of the people around him and in his appraisal and criticism of those problems in the context of the wide humanity and mankind. His assertion of the importance of man and human values above everything else is reflected in this novel through the farewell of Amit and Labanya. This novel is unique among the novels of Rabindranath Tagore on account of its difference from the rest in intent and content. Here the poet in Tagore once again dominates over the novelist. It is a "great love poem written in prose." It is popular among the readers and has won generous praise from mature critics. Krishna Kripalani accounts the reasons for its popularity as "its modern setting, its playful mocking tone, its challenging style, the author's trick of introducing himself as the butt of the hero's merciless criticism, the scintillating wit of the dialogue...."[82] Further, S.K. Banerjee is of the opinion that the novel is written in a "more consistent poetic strain and on a more purely poetic theme than perhaps any other novel in the world's history."[83] Dr. Sukumar Sen describes it as "a love story written as if to end all love stories."[84] Niharranjan Ray maintains that it is a "testament of love and beauty."[85] Dr. K.R.S. Iyengar expresses that "it is doubtless a witty and entertaining story, but it has also a core of serious purpose which lifts it high above the level of romantic comedy."[86]

It is a social romance with ironical undertones and an obvious dig at the new generation of social snobs. The title is reminiscent of the sentimental romances like the ones popularised by Mills and Boon, redolent of a romantic idealism which is rarely realisable in the every day world of harsh realities. Tagore seems to be parodying this class of literature which has such unfailing fascination for adolescent minds as well as those given to romanticising life itself. Such a view of the novel appears justified from the playful mocking tone of Tagore in the description of incident and character. The principal characters, when judged from their responses, seem to be enacting roles as in a romance rather than being propelled by any deeply felt emotions and this is the reason why there is no inconsolation of spirit or disintegration of personality even when their experience of love is marked by disappointments and even despair.

The fact that the outlook on love of the principal characters is conditioned by poetry, is indicative of their penchant for self-dramatisation and viewing of life through the delectable haze of romance. In other words, love stirs their imagination rather than their essential being. It is no wonder then that they rely on verse — whatever be its quality or source to make their points and that even their final farewells are couched in verse. The coming together of Amit and Labanya in the sylvan surroundings of Shillong thus has the appearance of a dream—a dream that cannot withstand the onset of reality, in the shape of Amit's former fiancee. It does not, however, mean that they are completely untouched by their experience of love, romanticised though it is. The novel, in fact, makes an attempt at probing the human situation beneath its poeticised facade which is what imparts to it an added significance. The novel, thus, has elements of humanism in its being both a parody of the conventional romance and a subtle comedy of romantic attitudes, gleefully rendered.

The novel begins with a scintillating description of the Calcutta smart set to which the hero, Amit, belongs. An affluent Oxford educated barrister, Amit is obsessed with "style." His deportment and speech are marked by a certain unnaturalness and unconventionality. What is remarkable is that he sets out to ridicule the high society with a dazzling display of non-conformity in dress and behaviour and a coruscating wit. He sports native dresses for not being in vogue among this set. He revels in shocking people with his smart sayings which are invariably contrary to popular beliefs. He derides democracy, rebuts the champions of feminism by declaring that the despotism of women will be more terrible than that of men and holds that no poet must poetise for more than five years from his twenty-fifth to his thirtieth year and hence that Tagore must yield his throne to others instead of continuing "perversely" for ever. Though he cultivates the fair sex, he is careful that his gallantry extends to all of them in order to produce an impression rather than evoke a response. His answer to proposals of matrimony is:

> The girl whom in my imagination I vainly court has no address. She hardly ever crosses a threshold. She flashes into my heart like a meteor from the sky and is lost in the air before she can enter brick—and mortar—abode.[87]

At the beginning of the story Amit Rai is seen as a clever and talented young man who exemplifies the very acme of sophistication and mental culture but whose proneness to romanticism and narcissism will prevent him, in the ultimate analysis, from manifesting any true love for any one.

Tagore's capacity for sarcasm and caricature is even more evident in his description of the ultra-modern females of Amit's set. Amit's two sisters, with their modish pet-names. Cissie and Lissie, are shown as having fully imbibed modern fashions in the following words:

> From head to heel they are absolutely the latest brand-smartly wrapped ware in the showcase of fashion. They fancy high heels and dangle over their lace-trimmed, low-cut blouses beads of amber and coral, while their saris cling and slant serpentwise across their limbs. They trip when they walk, and squeak when they talk, their laughter is measured in a crescendo of squeals: they tilt their heads smiling winsomely, daring quick sidelong glances: they can look soulful too (10).

Katie or Kettee Mitter (a fashionable contraction of Ketaki Mitra) is even more sophisticated. While at Oxford, she had become affianced to Amit but having lost all hopes of marriage with him, turned a flirt. Tagore gives a fine ironical sketch of her thus:

> ...In her spite against the average Bengali girl's pride in her long hair, she had with equal pride applied the scissors to her own, so that her hair, like the tail of a tadpole, had been transmuted into the bob of the evolved model. Her naturally fair complexion was well coated with enamel. In her childhood Katie's dark eyes had been gentle and serene, now they seemed too lofty to rest on the common place. If by chance they did rest, they took no notice: or , if they did take notice, they glittered like a half-drawn knife. Her lips, once sweet and unaffected, were set by constant sneering in the hard curve of a twisted goad.... Her blouse exposed rather than covered her bust and her bare arms would rest now on a table, now on the arm of a chair, or would be posed with the utmost care in an affectation of extreme refinement. When she puffed at a cigarette held between her manicured fingers, it was less for the sake of the smoke than for the decorative effort (100).

Katie's brother, Naren Mitter, a close friend of Amit, comes equally under Tagore's scorn. A self-proclaimed art-expert, he had spent many years abroad. Son of a rich Zamindar, he is now fully given to a frivolous, though fashionable life:

If he could not improve the art of painting, he could at least confound it. The ends of his moustache were carefully pointed upwards French fashion, and equally carefully was his shaggy hair neglected. He was handsome enough, but in the assiduous endeavour to make himself more so, he had loaded the dressing table with all sorts of Parisian beauty-aids. The equipment of his wash basin would have more than sufficed even for the ten-headed Ravana.... His English was well-seasoned with slang, which he minced and drawled with a sleepy, sluggish stare in his half-closed eyes. Those who knew testified how many blue-blooded nobles of England spoke in such muffled tones. Moreover, his stock of horsey slang and obscene oaths made him the hero of his set (99).

Amit, who hails from such a milieu described above may not be expected to evince any genuine love for any one. Nevertheless, the unexpected happens. Amit chooses Shillong for a holiday. Driving along a narrow, crooked road with his head full of Kalidasa's poetry, he dashes his car against an oncoming one. From the other car which is partially damaged emerges Labanya whose form is described as:

> Amit saw a rare vision, as though a Lakshmi had risen from the ocean which the gods had churned and stood poised above the foaming and raging waters. Had Amit seen this same girl in a city drawing-room, in the midst of half a dozen others, he might have noticed her but would have missed this revelation of the full splendour of her being (21).

Labanya, the lady in the car, had come to Shillong for summer along with Yogamaya, as a tutoress to her daughter, Surama. She had completed her M.A. and still retained her love of books. At one time she was in love with Sobhanlal, her father's student. A misunderstanding drove Sobhanlal away from her and when her father remarried, Labanya quitted her house determined to live on her own earnings. Whatever inclinations she felt towards love had been quelled by her sad experiences but her encounter now with Amit revives them. "In a moment Labanya was awake. At long last she was aware of herself" (33). This experience kindles her imagination but not her heart. Amit is fascinated not only by Labanya's beauty but also by her keen intellect. To his pleasant surprise, he discovers on her table, a volume of Donne's Poetical Works; Donne and his contemporaries had been the subject of his critical studies at Oxford. His ebulient and restless spirit finds solace in Labanya's tranquil serenity:

> Amit himself had intellect but no forbearance, judgment but no patience: he had read much and learnt much but of tranquility, he had achieved nothing. In Labanya's face he saw a picture of serenity, born not of emotional self-complacency but of the profound poise of a calm and balanced mind (37).

Labanya accepts his proposal of marriage because of Yogamaya's persuasion and Amit sends for an engagement ring from Calcutta. Labanya, is at first enchanted by the discovery of love and tends to dramatise it as much as Amit does. However, deep in her heart, she has reservations about him. She tells him: "When I listen to your words, I am overwhelmed with fear, Mita" (54).

Her reply to Amit's query as regards the basis for her fears is:

> I beg of you, do not wish to marry me.... You are not the one to set up a household. You are in quest of whatever will quench your fancy's thirst. That is why you flit from literature to literature and that is why you have come to me. Shall I speak the truth ? In your heart of hearts you consider marriage, as you are always calling it vulgar. (54-55)

Amit pleads that his outlook is bound to change after marriage but Labanya is certain that he loves not her but an idealised image of her in his mind. She tells Yogamaya:

> ...he does not want me.... With words he seeks to remould me.... I want to remain a dream as long as I may, blended with his words, with the play of his fancy. Indeed, why should I call it a dream, when it is for me a unique rebirth, a unique revelation of self in a unique world? (61).

But her doubts are dispelled by Amit's near-frenzied wooing and Yogamaya's pleadings; and soon she gives her consent for the marriage. They spend their time in fashioning a fanciful house for their life after marriage. There is an unexpected reversal; Amit's Calcutta set suddenly descends upon Shillong and this development has the effect of wrenching them from their dream world by bringing them into contact with reality which they have seemingly ignored.

On hearing Amit's romance his sisters and friends from Calcutta hurry to Shillong rather perturbed because the woman he has reportedly fallen in love with is a "governess." They are amused at how love had transformed the fastidious Amit into a rustic "swain." Since Amit is unwilling to enlighten them about his love, his sister Cissie and his former fiancee, Katie Mitter proceed to Yogamaya's house. As Katie is about to upbraid Labanya, Amit turns up with the ring that had arrived from Calcutta and as if to nullify Katie's rudeness, slips the ring on Labanya's finger. Katie reminds Amit about the ring he had given her seven years ago at Oxford and which she had not taken off for a single moment. She removes it, throws it on the table and storms out with tears pouring down her "enamelled" cheeks.

At this turn of events labanya expresses her distress. But Amit explains that Katie was an altogether different person then:

> Katie's face was not plastered with paint those days, her laughter was spontaneous, she could still blush (112).

But Labanya holds Amit responsible for the transformation of Katie into "a concentrated, superfine essence of foreign make" (100). She tells Amit:

> She once gave herself completely into your hands, Mita. Why didn't you make her your own? You loosened your hold and let her go, no matter why, and since then a dozen hands have fallen on her and made her what she is. It was because she lost you that she began to deck herself out for other tastes. That's why she looks like a foreign doll. If her heart had remained alive it couldn't have happened (114).

Labanya pleads with Amit to make amends for Katie and returns his ring saying that their inner bonds need no outward token. Amit understands the significance of this gesture and does not resist. The scene where Katie throws her ring on the table while "tears flow down her enamelled face" is unforgettable and indeed a turning-point in the story.

And Labanya? Tagore will provide for her too. The gentle, undemonstrative Shobhanlal, whom she had once rejected, has returned and sends a reticent letter. Labanya, chastened, accepts him. She has no bitterness over what has happened, not a word of censure for Amit. The last meeting is one of the loveliest things and she seems so much taller than Amit, who consoles himself with a poor analogy, of the pool and the water pot. Labanya's change is credible than Amit's whether his life with Katie would be happy in anybody's guess.

Amit sends a note of farewell to Labanya concluding with some lines from Rabindranath Tagore:

> Invisible, your image unchanging is in my eyes, in the unseen chamber of my heart you abide for ever (121).

The heroine has the last word. Along with the letter of invitation of her marriage with Sobhanlal, Labanya sends a reply to Amit in the form of a poem of a farewell:

> No loss is yours in losing me.
> An image of clay.
> If of that mortal dust
> You have fashioned a goddess.

Let the goddess remain for you to adore
With the evening star.
No gross touch of the actual me
Shall disturb the play of your worship,
No hot breath of ardour passion-lit
Sully its flowers, sacred, fragile,....
What I gave to you
Is yours by right everlasting.
O my princely, my peerless friend
What I gave to you was your own gift
The fuller your acceptance, the deeper my debt,
My friend, farewell (122)!

Thus the change in Labanya which makes room for Katie's marriage with Amit and her own marriage with Sobhanlal represents an aspect of Tagore's humanism involving man's sacrifice for the well-being of others along with his or her own fulfilment.

The novel is half playful and half earnest. The wistful parting at the end indicates that the love of Amit and Labanya had not been deep rooted; as in popular romances, they seem to have been more in love with love than with each other. So, there is no emotional struggle or upheaval involved in their farewells to each other; their separation leads to no laceration of spirit. B.C. Chakravorty comments that the transference of love is "mechanical and unconvincing."[88] There is also no "love's ascestism"[89] as noticed by Bhabani Bhattacharya nor is the "final note tragic,"[90] as supposed by Krishna Kripalani.

Whatever pangs of love are there, they are part of the self-dramatisation of the lovers, part of "a self-absorbed play of fancy."[91] Starting as a scorner of love, Amit comes under its enchantment in the romantic and Arcadian surroundings of Shillong but, after this fanciful and romantic phase, gets reconciled to a normal life with Ketaki. Labanya begins with a distrust of love but her romantic interlude with Amit helps her to respond to the devoted love of Sobhanlal. Tagore's artistic intention seems to be to mock playfully at those with a romantic turn of mind. Bhabani Bhattacharya also makes a fine remark that "such freshness, such youthfulness, could come from a writer in his seventieth year."[92]

To sum up, *Farewell, My Friend* is a novel based on Tagore's humanism which lays emphasis on the life and problems of the people around him; and the importance of man and human values above everything else as seen through the fond farewell of Amit and Labanya making rooms for his own marriage with Ketaki and Labanya's marriage with Sobhanlal.

(V) *TWO SISTERS*

"Rabindranath Tagore's short novel, *Two Sisters* is premised on the traditional and universal postulate of the dual image of woman as mother and beloved—a premise already projected by him in symbolic form in his poem entitled "*Two Women*":

> When the primeval ocean was churned, two divine forms
> emerged from the endless deep; One was Urvashi
> queen of the passions, temptress of the gods.
> The other was Lakshmi, maternal and pure,
> benefactress of all that lives and breathes.
> Urvashi brings with her the heady wine of April
> and bursts into the restless songs of youth.
> Her flaming revelry distracts all mortals
> and steals the peace from their hearts.
> Then comes Lakshmi, her eyes glistening with
> tears of affection. She soothes the passions
> and restores the serene joys of autumn,
> autumn with its fruitful maturity and repose.
> Her blessings bring perfection and plenty,
> and her gentle smile overflows with
> the nectar of grace.[93]

In the novella Tagore restates this views, minus the myth at the beginning. In fact, this novella seeks to perspectivise the seeming dualism through the two sisters, Sarmila and Urmimala, assigned respectively the roles of wife and beloved. Krishna

Kripalani also remarks that the novel is "mainly psychological in interest, dealing with the usual triangle, in this case, two sisters in love with the same man."[94] Tagore dwells on the theme of illicit love in this novella. As human problem—human interest, is the core of the theme, the novella represents Tagore's humanism based on his awareness of life and problems of the people around him and his love for earth and humanity.

This novella has not been warmly received by critics. Many regard it as a novel with the "most unconvincing story" and the weakest of Tagore's novels. However, Bhabani Bhattacharya remarks that though *Two Sisters* "may not be comparable to Tagore's best" yet it is "a work of art exquisite in its own individual fashion."[95]

The theme of *Two Sisters* is very simple. It deals with the problems of psychological maladjustment in married life. Sarmila marries Sasanka, an engineer. After a period of happy married life, her husband loses interest in her. He is vexed at her motherly affection and solitude for him. Just then, Sarmila falls sick and her sister Urmimala comes to attend on her. Sasanka falls in love with his sister-in-law, neglects his business and incurs heavy losses. Sarmila whose interest in life is the happiness of her husband, proposes that Sasanka should marry her sister as she feels that her husband cannot be happy without Urmi. But this situation is averted by Urmi's decision to go to Europe for further studies. This novella, therefore, ends with a weak attempt at reconciliation between husband and wife.

Sarmila is the embodiment of the maternal instinct. Nothing delights her as much as "mothering" her husband because she regards him as "utterly helpless and pathetically incapable of looking after his own physical needs—this impression was too firmly rooted in Sarmila's mind to be ever dislodged."[96] Her love is of an assuaging kind and she has all the attributes traditionally associated with Hindu womanhood; befitting modesty, selfless devotion, sacrificial spirit and self-effacement. But in Urmimala's case the contours of tradition are blurred by the changes brought about by Western education which has led to a loosening, however slight, of the norms of conduct of the Indian woman. By nature "full of vitality and liveliness" (36) the biological impulses of her youth—she is considerably younger than her sister find a free play in the changed social milieu. Thus, the two sisters represent aptly the two factors of female psyche—one, homely, restrained, bountiful, comforting and the other outgoing, glamorous, scintillating and provocative.

The novella seems to demonstrate the possibility of the embodiment of the two love-modes in the same person on the idealistic rather than the empirical level. As Krishna Kripalani remarks, "Human nature and society being what they are, a man cannot always have both and love is at best only a partial fulfilment."[97] Within this underlying framework, the frustrations, disappointments, and distractions involving the two sisters, Sarmila and Urmimala; and Sasanka are worked out. Their triangular relationship gains in social significance by being enacted within confines and constraints of the unchanging or perhaps unchangeable family structure of Hindu society.

The elder sister Sarmila, who is married to Sasanka, a Government engineer, is completely devoted to her husband. Being childless and with no hope of one, she transfers all her repressed affections to her husband who finds her fussing over him nearly unbearable. Being the mother kind, this role comes naturally to her. There is no aspect of his existence, whether at home or in office, which escapes her attention and solicitude. At times, he chafes at this rigid ordering of his life and remonstrates:

> For goodness's sake, get hold of some god or deity like that Chakravarty wife. It's too much for me to withstand your attentions all by myself. Sharing them with a god would make it easier. The gods can stand excesses, but man is frail (9).

Sarmila's solicitude for her husband goes beyond the domestic sphere. He knows, however, that he is utterly dependent on her for his comfort. When he is superseded in service by an inexperienced, young Englishman, he tries to keep his humiliation a secret from his wife but she finds it out and makes him resign his job forthwith and procures with her money a partnership for him in her uncle's construction firm.

Throwing himself headlong into his work unmindful of his wife's anxiety for his health and comfort, Sasanka is soon able to pay off her debt with interest and also build his own house. His success spurs him on to greater involvement with his business to the extent that he finds no time to attend his own birthday celebrations so lovingly planned by Sarmila. The novelist records Sarmila's emotional plane:

> Her devotion which was once offered directly to its object was now directed to its symbols—in looking after the house and the garden, in knitting a cover for Sasanka's sofa, embroidering flower patterns on his pillow-case, in setting on a corner of his coffee-table bouquets of tuberoses in blue crystal vases. It cost her no little pain to worship her deity from so great a distance (22).

When Sarmila falls ill suddenly and seriously, Sasanka who deeply loves her becomes distraught and decides to stay by her side. Even this comfort is denied to her. Knowing as she does that her husband's happiness lies in his work, she urges him to return to his business. Even in sickness, her anxiety is for his comfort and not trusting the servants, she tries to arrange things for him herself. This only worsens her condition and in desperation she appeals to her sister, Urmimala, to come and take charge of the house:

> Never mind your college for a few days—come to the rescue of his household, otherwise I can't even die in peace (53).

Full of youth and vitality, Urmimala revealed to Sasanka a type of woman he had never known. His newly awakened sense of masculine strength was fascinated by her essentially feminine nature. Really speaking, she exemplifies the feminine fervour of the beloved kind. Hailing from an affluent, aristocratic, and progressive family, she is allowed full scope to develop her animated and sprightly personality. The novelist portrays her behaviour:

> Good-looking as Urmimala was, she seemed even better looking than she was: the luminous intensity of her mind scintillated in the lively moments of her body. She was eager about everything; interested in science...ran out to the verandah to watch a wedding party pass by, with its bridegroom and the fanfare of trumpets; ...played tennis; was particularly good at badminton.... She dressed simply but elegantly; knew how to bring out the full beauty of the figure in a sari by a slight turn here, a right twist there, a little tightening here and a little loosening there.... She could play on the sitar.... She was never in want of a topic for conversation, never waited for a proper excuse for laughter. She had an inexhaustible talent for creating company out of dullness and filling emptiness with her mere presence (34-36).

Sasanka playfully suggests that the name Vidyut-lata (lightning-creeper) will be more appropriate for her.

Urmimala's father wants to found a hospital in memory of his son Hemanta who died after much painful medical treatment. So his second daughter, the vivacious Urmi is betrothed to Dr. Nirad Mukherjee, a prig if ever there was one. Nirad, who takes "a particular delight in running down those in whom the exuberance of youth was self-evident" (31), sets about to "reform" her by prescribing a rigid code of conduct. Urmi who yearns for romance chafes under the restraints imposed on her by her fiance. She wonders:

> Nirad merely directed her—why did he never for a moment woo her? For such an expression of ardour on his part her heart ever waited, and for want of it, remained unfulfilled; her very acts of duty became dry and lifeless (39).

Urmi tries hard to abide by the rigid code of conduct laid down by Dr. Nirad when he leaves for Europe for higher studies in medicine. But she does not find it easy. It is in this frame of mind that she is called upon to assist Sarmila in running her household in Sasanka's house.

The novelist has made it evident that Sasanka and Urmi are Kindred spirits even before Urmi's arrival in Sasanka's house. In the presence of Urmi the dedicated engineer Sasanka becomes a changed man—light-hearted, prankish and irrepressible, an aspect of his nature which is otherwise dormant. It is this very naughtiness of his that draws Urmi to him. "Her own irresponsible girlishness surged up in her when she was with him, and he too was no less a victim of her pranks" (44).

In the company of Urmi in the house, Sasanka experiences "the buoyancy of a playful, holiday spirit in the atmosphere"(59) and despite the heavy responsibility of his work, begins to spend more time at home. Life becomes a long round of pleasure for them—shopping, picnicking, playing tennis and indulging in tomfooleries. Urmi receives a letter from Dr. Nirad that he is getting married to a European woman, and so she feels free to devote herself to enjoyment. Sarmila's devoted affection could not hold Sasanka in the home. From her sickbed she helplessly watches him:

> Looking into Sasanka's face she could see that he was always in a kind of trance. That this mere slip of a girl should in a few days have shaken that stern worker out of his arduous striving—the ignominy was more agonising to Sarmila than the actual pain of her disease. (67)

However, her husband's happiness is the main ambition of her life. So she chooses to keep quiet. And her such act represents Tagore's humanism based on one's sacrifice for the well-being of other fellow beings.

Very soon, wrapped up in his enjoyment of fun with Urmi, Sasanka has grossly neglected his business, leaving it in the hands of one Jawaharlal who appropriates everything to himself. Sasanka is now faced with a colossal loss and has to sell everything, including the house to pay off his commitments. Now Urmi realises the havoc she has caused by her thoughtless conduct in weaning away her brother-in-law from his business:

> ....This terrible picture of her infatuation rose full and clear before her eyes. Instantly she flung herself at her sister's feet and began to repeat in hoarse and broken tones: Kick me away from your house, drive me away from your presence, now, this very minute (86).

But, Sarmila knows that this is impossible as she realises that her husband cannot afford to lose Urmi for whose sake he had risked the ruin of his business. In fact, it had been her consolation in her sickness that if she were to die, Urmi would be there to take her place. But, to her dismay, she recovers her health and this leads to a dilemma which she proposes to resolve by uniting Sasanka and Urmi in marriage: after all such an arrangement—"for sisters to be co-wives" (94)—is not unknown in Hindu society. To avoid any social scandal they could migrate to Nepal where Sasanka had once been offered a job. Urmi first consents but makes a French leave for Europe for higher studies in medicine to fulfil her father's ambition of founding hospital. In her farewell letter to Sasanka, she writes:

> I am on my way to Bombay *en route* for Europe. I shall carry out father's wishes and return a doctor in about six or seven years' time. In the meantime the havoc I have caused in your home will have had time to repair itself. Don't worry about me. I can't help worrying about you (99).

In another letter, begging the forgiveness of her sister, she writes:

> Didi, a thousand pranaams at your feet. Forgive me the wrong I have done you unwittingly. If no wrong has been

> done then that very knowledge will make me happy. I dare not hope for any greater happiness, nor indeed do I know for certain wherein lies happiness. If happiness is not in store for me, let it be so. Let me only not err (99).

The novella concludes with Sasanka's determination to revive his fortunes.

It is seen that *Two Sisters* is predicated on the two idealised images of womanhood as mother and sweet-heart. But this does not, in Srikumar Banerjee's opinion, make it "altogether theory-ridden."[98] Here Tagore is concerned with the presentation in human terms of the two postulates of womanly personhood. He has succeeded in creating flesh and blood characters, who, while remaining true to their symbolic image, exhibit the qualities of living beings as well. In health and sickness, in prosperity and adversity, Sarmila exhibits the same maternal solicitude and forgiving love for both her husband and her sister. Her such trait is expressed in Nirad's words:

> Sarmila—didi's love is serene and deep; and her care and devotion are like an act of religious merit; her duty knows no holiday (44).

Further, Sarmila exemplifies the view that "...the natural grace and sweetness of woman, her inborn wealth of love are sufficient in themselves for the fulfilment of her function in this world" (67). She embodies the qualities of devotion, service, self-effacement and self-abnegation. Tagore believes that true love demands sacrifice and forgiveness. Such people are ultimately rewarded by God with happiness and contentment. And this is the blossoming of the flower of Tagore's humanism.

On the other hand, the quality of Urmimala's love can be judged from its impact on Sasanka:

> Sasanka's mind was in a delirium of exhilaration. He felt transported to a fairy land where all sense of responsibility faded in a stupor of happiness (91).

At the end of the novella Urmimala becomes sobered but in

consonance with her nature and temperament opts for an independent life which has the effect of resolving the crisis befalling the characters. She is portrayed merely as a contrast to her sister, Sarmila, the protagonist of the novella.

To sum up, the novella seems to suggest that the two love modes are basically different and unbridgeable at least in the world of everyday realities. Further, it also points out that the combination of the two aspects of "mother" and "sweetheart" in one woman is an unattainable ideal. Thus human problem of love forms the core of theme and as such the novella represents Tagore's humanism.

(VI) *THE GARDEN*

Rabindranath Tagore's novella, *The Garden*, written about five years after *Farewell, My Friend* depicts humanism in its being an insightful study of the pathology of jealousy and possessiveness which drains a person of all feelings of love and generosity. "Illicit love and awakening of a new passion in the heart of a married man is painted with stark realism and without the saving grace of compassion."[99] In it "we have a sharp study of love and jealousy exploding in the death of the sick embittered wife."[100] The theme of the novel, illicit love, is not very original. Tagore has not cared to portray the inward conflict in the major characters, though the story is remarkable for its intense dramatic interest. Niharranjan Ray remarks:

> Malancha (*The Garden*) should have been written as a drama. The complete detachment and impersonality, the absence of all personal comment, the preponderance of dialogue, the quick tempo of events, such qualities as characterise this short novel, go better with the drama form.[101]

Krishna Kripalani is also of the same opinion. The story content of the novel is similar to that of *Two Sisters* but it has a different ending. In both these novels, the story is about the illicit love of middle-aged husband with a relation. In both, the wife falls sick and is confined to bed. But the two novels differ in one respect. In *Two Sisters,* Sasanka loves his wife till the end in spite of his flirtations with his sister-in-law, whereas in *The Garden,* Aditya ceases to love his sick wife when he falls in love with Sarala. Further, Sarmila never participates in her husband's work but only attends on him, whereas Niraja helps her husband in his work.

The novel is a study in the obsessive and neurotic psychology of a sick woman nursing the nightmares of loneliness and lovelessness. There is calamity when one grows too possessive of any dear object to suffer even the thought of deprivation from it. Tagore uses flashback technique in recalling Niraja's idyllic life with her florist husband, Aditya. So long as she is engaged in the garden work, the seeds of jealousy in her lie dormant but startling changes appear in her as she is separated from the garden by sudden illness. The garden was a source of emotional sustenance to her and alienation from it spells for her emotional impoverishment and spiritual sterility. Her physical separation from the garden due to her illness occasions the induction of Sarala a young relation of Aditya. Niraja looks upon this new entry as a Satanic intervention to blast her Edenic existence with her husband. Now her innate possessive instincts have gradually eroded her capacity for love and generosity.

Apart from the overtones of the Christian concept of Eden, the emblem of the garden traditionally connotes harmony of spirit and innocence of mind. As long as Niraja was healthy and active, she basked in the love of Aditya, whose name signifies the sun, the source of all life and light. Separation from the garden which would mean separation from active association with him, would make Niraja (meaning flower) wither away like a plant which is denied sunlight to die. Here lies the symbolic significance of the title of the novelette. This novelette may be viewed in humanist perspective on the basis of its theme centring round human problems, human behaviour and human nature.

Niraja is seen spending her moments in nostalgic recollections of her blissful past as she is paralysed in her sickbed. Ten years ago, Aditya, a famed florist had fallen in love with her and married her. Discerning his utter dedication to the garden, she identified herself with his work as she did not like the garden to intervene between her and Aditya. Enjoying her companionship and extolling her as his "Banalakshmi" Aditya tells Niraja:

> ...Along the path which your feet tread everyday, the flowers bloom on both sides, the spring breeze is drunk with your wine and the roses are delicious.... If you were not there, this my heaven of flowers would become mammon's market place. It's my good fortune that in the elysium of my life you are the goddess.[102]

As they are childless for a long time their married life finds ever new expressions of joy in the beauty of flower and leaf. In course of time, Niraja develops an attitude of possessiveness towards the garden, particularly the orchid House which she wants to be exclusively dedicated to her and her husband. That she is by nature jealous is evident by her attitude to Sarala whenever she is invited to participate in the planting festivities of each season. Aditya owed his fame and success as a florist to Sarala's uncle and they had grown up together in the uncle's garden. This knowledge becomes impalatable to Niraja who cannot tolerate her husband praising Sarala's skill in gardening. She would often resort to a mean trick to embarrass her by picking out an obscure botanical name from a book and innocently asking Sarala about it. When she faltered in her reply, Niraja would burst out into laughter and exclaim; "How clever! Even a child knows that it's called Cassia Javanica.... Even my Hala Mali could have told you that" (156).

However, this streak of jealousy does not become fully pronounced in the harmonious surroundings of the garden. So Aditya gets no inkling of it. Reigning supreme in her paradise, she cannot think of Sarala as a rival. Her cup of happiness becomes full when she conceives. But, complications arise at the time of delivery and the child has to be sacrificed to save the mother. Niraja's spirit turns completely sour and embittered and from this time onward she becomes bed-ridden.

As Niraja had been accustomed to the joyful routine of gardening, the sick room becomes to her a prison and a place for torture. Seeing her husband, through the window, in the company of Sarala who has been inducted into the garden, her jealousy knows no bound. She tries to belittle and humiliate her in the presence of her husband, servants and malis. Regarding her jealousy Krishna Kripalani remarks:

> More tragic than her physical misfortune is its effect on her mind. She who was generous when she was happy becomes unjust and vindictive when deprived of her happiness.[103]

Niraja's frustrations at being dissociated from the garden have dried up the very springs of her humanity and have filled her mind with insane jealousy. Tagore probes her gradually withering soul skilfully and provides her some lucid moments when she can objectively view her irrational conduct. She encourages the head Mali in his backbiting of Sarala against whom he complains to her for winning favour, possibly a reward. But on his departure, she groans:

> I've grown petty and mean.... My mind has shrunk to the level of Hala Mali's.... As ill luck would have it, I am crippled physically. But why this crippling of the mind as well? (141).

Sarala's name and presence are closely linked with Niraja's psychoneurotic manifestations. Niraja flares up the moment she sees Sarala and she reminds her husband how she had cherished the garden till it had become almost her very self. Now she cannot tolerate Sarala supplanting her and so reproaches her husband Aditya:

> ....Today I have seen another enter this very garden with impurity. ...Could you have borne to cut open my flesh

> and lodge someone else's spirit in it?.... Because you love her more than you love me. You hid it from me all along (157).

Stunned by these words Aditya replies:

> ...Niru, you have known me for ten years in joy and sorrow, in all kinds of work. If after that you can bring yourself to say such words as those, I have no answer to give (157-58).

But, Niraja, in her lucid intervals, feels that she is being vindictive and becomes penitent. And begging forgiveness from her husband she says:

> I've been unjust to Sarala.... Forgive me for what has happened. Only love me, love me, and I'll do whatever you say (185).

Sarala's succumbing to jealousy is made by her husband. In fact, Aditya bears a curiously passive attitude towards his physically and emotionally disintegrating wife. He appears to be so naive as not to comprehend that his praise of Sarala before Niraja only aggravates her suffering. Niraja's accusation of infidelity on his part rouses his dormant love for Sarala and without hesitation he openly expresses it to her:

> .....I love you. It fills my heart with joy that I can say this today so easily and truthfully. What was hidden all these twenty-three years in the bud has, thank God, blossomed forth to-day. I tell you, I could be a coward and untrue to myself to suppress it.... Oh, why was I so blind ? Why didn't I see you as you are? Why did I blunder into this marriage? (165).

Like Niraja, Aditya too seems to be self-centred though to a lesser degree and gets indifferent to his wife's physical and mental anguish.

Circumstances have cast Sarala into the role of "the other woman" and her dramatic function is to release the baser emotions of Niraja. Her spirit of self-abnegation and sacrifice is revealed in the way she patiently bears the teasing and taunting act of Niraja and nurses her with tenderness and love.

To quote the novelist:

> She knew the pain that gnawed at Niraja's heart. All the void in the heart of this childless mother had been filled by this garden and today after ten long years she was an exile from it, though so near it. Before her very eyes it was torn away from her (140).

This sympathy in Sarala for the physically paralysed and mentally agonised Niraja represents an aspect of Tagore's humanism which involves man's love of fellow man and his thinking for the good of mankind. Another aspect of humanism is seen in Sarala's courting arrest as a freedom fighter and going into the prison. She has done it just to nourish the disintegrated mental state of Niraja because she knew that her presence in the garden would be a constant thorn in Niraja's mind. Before leaving for prison, Sarala appeals to Aditya:

> Swear by me that you will give yourself unstintingly and fill the last few days of Didi's life with happiness. Make her forget altogether that I had ever been here to break the brimming vessel of her fortune (178).

Now Niraja seems to regain her energy and senses in the absence of Sarala. It is remarkable as it is significant how her convulsions of pain earlier were brought about by Sarala's very appearance or even by a mention of her name. Bracing herself she informs her husband:

> Do you mean to say that because I am bedridden my garden too must be a sick bed? ....I'll myself direct him (the mali) from this sickbed and you'll see the face of the garden change in the couple of days (182).

Realising that Sarala is now away in prison, she even seems to feel kindly about her and assures her husband thus:

> Since last night I've vowed again and again when I see her next I'll take her in my arms with a clean heart, as if

> she were my own sister. You must help me to carry out this last vow of mine. Promise me that I shall always have your love; then I shall be able to give mine to every one before I die (185).

Niraja's distrust and possessive jealousy have brought about her own psychosomatic kind of illness and suffering. It is clearly seen and in order to relieve her from such illness one of her relatives advises her to cultivate the spirit of generosity in the following words:

> Let me tell you something, Boudi. As long as you imagine that someone is robbing you of your treasure, a fire will consume your ribs. You will have no peace. But just pull yourself together, and say for once, "Let me give! Let me give away what I hold most dear to him whom I hold most dear," and in an instant the burden will be lifted off you and your heart will brim over with happiness.... Just say, right now, "I give, I give, I give up everything, I keep back nothing. Unattached, untainted, I am ready to depart; no tangle of regret shall I leave behind on earth" (170-71).

For some time Niraja appears to free herself from her intense subjectivity but the news of Sarala's release from prison brings about a relapse and as soon as Sarala herself appears before her, she falls a victim to a violent paroxysm of jealousy which proves fatal. The last scene is presented in a highly dramatic manner and so it deserves to be quoted in full:

> Sarala entered and bent down to take the dust of her feet. At the touch of her hand Niraja's whole body, recoiled convulsively as if struck by lightning. Automatically the feet were jerked aside. In a broken voice she cries out, "I can't, I can't, I can't give, I can't." As she spoke an unnatural strength seemed to possess her. The dilated pupils of her eyes glittered. Grasping Sarala's hand, she shrieked, "No room for you here, you witch of hell, no room for you. I'll stick on, stick on, stick on, stick on!"

> Suddenly a pale, emaciated figure in chemise leapt out of the bed and stood erect. An unnatural voice hissed, "Get out at once, or everyday my danger shall pierce your breast. I'll drain you off the last drops of your blood."
>
> She fell to the floor. At the sound of her voice Aditya rushed into the room...with the last words Niraja's last strength had been spent. All was still (187).

Though the novelette does not deive deep into the deeper and profounder aspects of Niraja's despair, it does show that "No tragedy is greater than the poverty of spirit which paralyses our capacity to love and to forgive."[104]

Thus the climactic scene comes as a fitting close to the morbid career of a psychosomatic who is plunged into an abyss of destruction of self through frustration born of deprivation. The novel ends with the ghastly and horrible death of Niraja. It is true as Niharranjan Ray remarks:

> In "Dui Bon" (*Two Sisters*) the author's sympathy for Sarmila is clear and unmistakable but for Niraja in "Malancha" (*The Garden*) he seems to have none; she attracts no love; no admiration, even no sympathy.[105]

Though Niraja and Aditya appear to be leading outwardly a blissful existence in a delightful garden, they are in essence self-centred and possessive. Niraja is grasping in her passion for the garden and her husband Aditya is weak and egocentric. Consequently, Sarala's entry has reduced their facade of love to shambles. Their sanctuary cannot be sustained without the qualities of sacrifice and self-subordination which are the life breath of true love.

To sum up, the novelist is severe and unsympathetic towards the characters of the novel and the whole atmosphere is filled with cruelty. It may be, as Humayun Kabir finds, due to "Tagore's sense of frustration and disillusionment"[106] caused by lack of funds to Visva Bharati and the indifferent attitude of the people towards his message of sanity in politics. He is hinting at the idea that superstition and narrowness have been gaining ground on all sides. And with this is revealed his humanism which is visible in his awareness of life and problems of the people around him and in his appraisal and criticism of those problems in the context of the wide humanity and mankind.

REFERENCES

1. George Sampson, *The Concise Cambridge History of English Literature,* rev. by R.C. Churchill (1970, rpt. London: Cambridge Univ. Press, 1975), 741.
2. Bhabani Bhattacharya, "Tagore as a Novelist" in *Rabindranath Tagore: 1861-1961, A Centenary Volume* (New Delhi: Sahitya Akademi, 1961), 96.
3. Niharranjan Ray, "Three Novels of Tagore: Chokher Bali, Gora, Yoga Yoga" in *Indian Literature IV* (1961), 165.
4. Humayun Kabir, *Rabindranath Tagore: Tagore Lectures 1961* (London: School of Oriental and African Studies, 1961), 17.
5. V.S. Naravane, *An Introduction to Rabindranath Tagore* (Madras: Macmillan, 1977), 117.
6. *Ibid.*, 118.
7. Masti Venkatesa Iyengar, *Rabindranath Tagore.* Bangalore: Jeevan Karyalaya, 1946, 92.
8. Krishna Kripalani, *Rabindranath Tagore*: A Biography. London: Oxford Univ. Press, 1962.
9. R.C. Majumdar (E.D.) *The History and Culture of Indian People—Struggle for Freedom* Vol. XI, Bombay: Bharatiya Vidya Bhavan, 1969, 916-19.
10. Krishna Kripalani, *Rabindranath Tagore: A Biography,"* 188.
11. Humayun Kabir, *The Bengali Novel.* Calcutta: Firma K.L. Mukhopadhyay, 1968, 34.
12. K.R. Srinivasa Iyengar, "A General Survey," in *The Novel In Modern India,* ed. Iqbal Baktiyar (Bombay: The P.E.N. All India Centre, 1961), 11.
13. Mohit Chakrabarti, *Rabindranath Tagore*: *Diverse Dimensions,* (New Delhi: Atlantic Publishers & Distributors, 1990), 160.
14. Krishna Kripalani, *Binodini,* (New Delhi: Sahitya Akademi, 1968), VI.
15. *Ibid.*, 24.
16. *Ibid.*, 34.
17. *Ibid.*, 25.

18. *Ibid.*, 25.
19. *Ibid.*, 98.
20. *Ibid.*, 49.
21. *Ibid.*, 89.
22. *Ibid.*, 135.
23. *Ibid.*, 136.
24. *Ibid.*, 37.
25. *Ibid.*, 42.
26. *Ibid.*, 67 (emphasis added).
27. Srikumar Banerjee, "Rabindranath's Novels" in *Homage to Rabindranath Tagore*, ed. B.M. Chaudhuri (Kharagpur: Indian Institute of Technology, 1961), 73.
28. *Binodini*, 132.
29. *Ibid.*, 62.
30. Kabir, Humayun, *The Bengali Novel*, 36.
31. *Binodini*, 39.
32. *Ibid.*, 51.
33. *Ibid.*, 53.
34. *Ibid.*, 60.
35. *Ibid.*, 107.
36. *Ibid.*, 132.
37. *Ibid.*, 132.
38. *Ibid.*, 140
39. *Ibid.*, 143.
40. Bimanbehari Majumdar, *Heroines of Tagore*. Calcutta: Firma K.L. Mukhopadhyay, 1968, 212.
41. *Binodini*, 217.
42. *Ibid.*, 218.
43. Bimanbehari Majumdar, *Heroines of Tagore*, 126.
44. Niharranjan Ray, "Three Novels of Tagore," in *Indian Literature, Tagore* Number, 169.
45. Niharranjan Ray, *An Artist in Life* (Trivandrum University of Kerala, 1967), 186.
46. Krishna Kripalani, *Rabindranath Tagore: A Biography* (London: Oxford University Press, 1962), 188.
47. Mukherjee, S., *Passage to America* (Calcutta: Bookland Pvt. Ltd., 1964), 54.

48. Lesny V., quoted by Krishna Kripalani, *Rabindranath Tagore: A Biography* (London: Oxford University Press, 1962), 199.
49. Sengupta, S.C., *The Great Sentinel* (Calcutta: A. Mukherjee, 1948), 204.
50. Ray, Niharranjan, *An Artist in Life* (Trivandrum: University of Kerala, 1967), 186.
51. Chakravorty, B.C., *Rabindranath Tagore: His Mind and Art* (New Delhi: Young India Publications, 1971), 193.
52. Iyengar, Masti Venkatesa, *Rabindranath Tagore* (Bangalore: Jeevan Karyalaya, 1946).
53. Mukherjee, S., *Passage to America* (Calcutta: Bookland Pvt. Ltd., 1964), 179.
54. Edward Thompson, *Rabindranath Tagore: His Life and Work*, rev. by Kalidas Nag (Calcutta: Y.M.C.A. Publishing House, 1961), 31.
55. Krishna Kripalani, *Rabindranath Tagore: A Biography*, 200.
56. Humayun Kabir, *The Bengali Novel* (Calcutta: Firma K.L. Mukhopadhyay, 1968), 40.
57. *The Wreck*, transl. J.G. Drummond (rpt. Madras: Macmillan, 1990), 6. All subsequent references in parentheses are to this edition.
58. Srikumar Banerjee, "Rabindranath's Novels" in *Homage to Rabindranath Tagore*, 73.
59. B.C. Chakravorty, *Rabindranath Tagore: His Mind and Art*, 193.
60. Krishna Kripalani, *Rabindranath Tagore: A Biography*, 199.
61. M.M. Bhattacharjee, *Rabindranath Tagore: Poet and Thinker*, (Delhi: Kitab Mahal, 1961), 96.
62. K. Gopal, *Social Thought of Rabindranath Tagore* (Meerut: Arun Prakashan, 1974), 56.
63. Humayun Kabir, *The Bengali Novel*, 40.
64. Dr. A.V. Krishna Rao, *The Novels of Rabindranath Tagore*, (Triveni: Quarterly, July' 64.)
65. Sengupta, S.C., *The Great Sentinal* (Calcutta: A. Mukherjee and Co., 1948), 212.
66. Kabir, Humayun, *The Bengali Novel* (Calcutta: Firma K.L. Mukhopadhyay, 1968), 46.
67. Tagore, Rabindranath, *Chaturanga*, Trans. Ashok Mitra, (New Delhi: Sahitya Akademi, 1963). All subsequent references in parentheses are to the second translation.
68. Ray, Niharranjan, *An Artist in Life* (Trivandrum: University of Kerala, 1967), 233.

69. Sengupta, S.C., *The Great Sentinel*, 212.
70. Kripalani, Krishna, *Rabindranath Tagore: A Biography* (London: Oxford University Press, 1963), 250.
71. Kabir, Humayun, *The Bengali Novel*, 46.
72. Mitra, Ashok, Trans. *Chaturanga* (New Delhi: Sahitya Akademi, 1963), 7-8.
73. Kabir, Humayun, *The Bengali Novel*, 48.
74. Raj, G.V., *Tagore: The Novelist*, (New Delhi: Sterling Publishers Private Limited, 1983), 64.
75. Kripalani, Krishna, *Rabindranath Tagore: A Biography* (London: Oxford University Press, 1962), 250.
76. Banerjee, Srikumar, "Rabindranath's Novels" in *Homage to Rabindranath Tagore*, ed. B.M. Chandhuri (Kharagpur: Indian Institute of Technology, 1961), 80.
77. Kripalani, Krishna, *Rabindranath Tagore: A Biography*, (London: Oxford University Press, 1962), 251.
78. Iyenyar, Masti Venkatesa, *Rabindranath Tagore* (Bangalore: Jeevan Karyalaya, 1946), 118.
79. Sengupta, S.C., *The Great Sentinel*, 216.
80. *Ibid.*, p. 216.
81. Ray, Niharranjan, *The Artist in Life*, 232.
82. Kripalani, Krishna, *Rabindranath Tagore: A Biography* (London: Oxford University Press, 1962), 334.
83. Quoted in Kripalani, Krishna, *Rabindranath Tagore: A Biography*, 335.
84. *Ibid.*, 335.
85. Ray, Niharranjan, *An Artist in Life* (Trivandrum: University of Kerala, 1968), 281.
86. Iyengar, Dr. K.R.S., *Rabindranath Tagore* (New Delhi: Sterling Publishers Private Limited, 1987), 85.
87. *Farewell, My Friend*, Transl. Krishna Kripalani from *Sesher Kavita* (1929). (London: The New India Publishing Company, 1946; 1956, rpt. Bombay: Jaico Publishing House, 1966), 12. All subsequent references in parentheses are to this edition.
88. Chakravorty, B.C., *Rabindranath Tagore: His Mind and Art* (New Delhi: Young India Publications, 1971), 215.
89. Bhattacharya, Bhabani, "Tagore as a Novelist" in *Rabindranath Tagore: A Centenary Volume* (New Delhi: Sahitya Akademi, 1961), 100.

90. Kripalani, Krishna, *Rabindranath Tagore: A Biography* (London: Oxford University Press, 1962), 334.
91. Banerjee, Srikumar, "Rabindranath's Novels" in *Homage to Rabindranath Tagore,* ed. B.M. Chaudhuri (Kharagpur: Indian Institute of Technology, 1961), 82.
92. Bhattacharya, Bhabani, *op. cit.*, 100.
93. Raj, G.V., *Tagore: The Novelist,* (New Delhi: Sterling Publishers Pvt. Ltd., 1983), 82.
94. Kripalani, Krishna, *Rabindranath Tagore: A Biography* (London: Oxford University Press, 1962), 372.
95. Bhattacharya, Bhabani, "Tagore as a Novelist" in *Rabindranath Tagore: A Centenary Volume,* ed. by S. Radhakrishnan (New Delhi: Sahitya Akademi, 1961), 101.
96. *Two Sisters,* transl. by Krishna Kripalani from *Dui Bon* (1933), (1945; rpt. Calcutta: Visva–Bharati, 1964), 55. All Subsequent references are to this edition.
97. Kripalani, Krishna, *Rabindranath Tagore: A Biography,* 372.
98. Banerjee, Srikumar, "Rabindranath's Novels" *Homage to Rabindranath Tagore,* ed. B.M. Chaudhuri (Kharagpur: Indian Istitute of Technology, 1961), 83.
99. Kabir, Humayun, *The Bengali Novel* (Calcutta: Firma K.L. Mukhopadhyay, 1968), 52.
100. Iyengar Srinivasa, K.R., *Rabindranath Tagore* (New Delhi: Sterling Publishers Pvt. Ltd. 1987), 86.
101. Ray, Niharranjan, *An Artist in Life* (Trivandrum: University of Kerala, 1967), 283.
102. *The Garden,* Transl. Krishna Kripalani from *Malancha* (1934). Included in *Farewell, My Friend* and *The Garden* (1956, rpt. Bombay: Jaico Publishing House, 1966), 146. All subsequent references in parentheses are to the English translation.
103. Kripalani, Krishna, *Rabindranath Tagore: A Biography* (London: Oxford University Press, 1962), 373.
104. Kripalani, Krishna, *Rabindranath Tagore: A Biography,* 373.
105. Ray, Niharranjan, *An Artist in Life,* 284.
106. Kabir, Humayun, *The Bengali Novel,* 53.

4

Tagore's English Novels: Critical Appraisal in Nationalist Perspectives

(VII) *GORA*

Gora, the longest and the most widely acclaimed novel of Rabindranath Tagore, has the theme of nationalism needed in a multi-racial and multi-religious community like India. It exemplifies Tagore's vision of new, syncretistic India, rising above the considerations of caste, community and race. At the beginning the central character Gora seemed to be a bigoted and xenophobic Hindu nationalist. But, he undergoes a process of realisation of his ideals and achieves a liberal humanistic ethics at the end. So the novel has contemporary relevance. It is really a strong political and patriotic novel voicing the aspirations of the resurgent India. The central theme of the novel has a political undercurrent. The novel reflects the patriotic zeal of Gora and also projects all the important political questions, the conflict of the ideals and aspiration between the East and the West. In the character of Gora "Tagore has tried to bring about the fusion of the East and the West."[1] The novel, covering a wide canvas, marks Tagore's "search for national identity."[2] It also represents his efforts "at projecting an image of India which is, at once, historical and ahistorical."[3] It is, "perhaps the most complete picture of the life of Bengal towards the end of the last century."[4]

The novel has an epical sweep which has tempted more than one critic to compare or equate it with the Indian *Mahabharata* or Tolstoy's *War and Peace*. Niharranjan Ray feels that "*Gora* has the amplitude of the ancient epic,"[5] and Sukumar Sen has viewed it "as...something like a *Mahabharata* of modern India."[6] Annada Sankar Ray considers it "the greatest novel ever written in India."[7] Krishna Kripalani designates it as "the epic of India in transition"[8] and, with some qualifications, equates it with "*War and Peace.*"[9] Bhabani Bhattacharya finds that "Gora is contemporary and yet timeless" as is the case with many great literary works of the world and "it reaches out towards the universal."[10]

Various factors contribute to make *Gora* a popular novel of grand scale. Firstly, it is "the only novel in Bengali which mirrors faithfully the social, political and cultural life of the entire educated Bengali middle Class."[11] Secondly, it does not suffer from the poetic excesses of Tagore's other novels. Thirdly, the whole novel is filled with polemics which are not found in his other novels. As Krishna Kripalani feels, the presence of polemics in such a book is "Inevitable in view of its very theme, the author does not lose the thread of the main narrative whose interest is sustained to the end."[12] Fourthly, it is the only work of Tagore where the life of the city of Calcutta forms an integral part of the story. Fifthly, the novel reveals to us Tagore's transition from nationalism to internationalism. Sixthly, nowhere else does Tagore use such a wide canvas, massive design, number of episodes and big galaxy of life-like characters. The most interesting factor is that for the first time in the novels of Tagore, a male character dominates the action. Nowhere else do we find a character like Gora "so masculine in the whole of Tagore's writings."[13] In no other novel does Tagore describe the Brahmo-Hindu conflicts and their fanaticism. No wonder then, *Gora,* is given the highest place in literature not only for its intellectual content or debates or its historical association but for its "skilful disposition of events, its masterly delineation of characters, the solid nature of its content and craft."[14]

In spite of the above claims and comparisons, *Gora* lacks the awesome background and titanic struggle which could lend it an epic dimension. However, it depicts a momentous period in Indian history when Hindu society was desperately striving to prevent its own disintegration in the face of challenges from within and without. What the novel brings out is the predicament of an active consciousness, exemplified in the protagonist, Gora who is driven to desperate straits in responding to the stimulus of orthodox revivalism on the one hand, and liberal reformism on the other; a predicament which seems inevitable in the case of any nation or society caught up in the march of historical evolution.

The tensions generated among the Bengali middle-class, the Hindu-Brahmo controversy and the stirrings of national consciousness towards the end of the last century have created the historical and social setting for *Gora*. In the first half of the nineteenth century, under the impact of Western thought and education, some young men in Bengal joined the Christian missionaries in an outright condemnation and ridicule of Hinduism. Raja Ram Mohan Roy founded the Brahmo Samaj (1828) which renounced all meaningless superstitions and taboos and aimed at a synthesis of the best in all faiths. In the course of time the Brahmo Samaj acquired a rigid anti-Hindu bias, trying to demolish as it were the foundations of Hindu faith. Alarmed by the attacks of Christian missionaries and Brahmo Samajists on their faith, orthodox Hindus started organising themselves into such revivalist groups as Dharma Sabha (1830), the Arya Samaj (1875), and the Ramakrishna Mission (1898). The Hindu revivalist upsurge acted as stimulus for the nascent nationalism with its emphasis on self-respect and preservation of tradition. *Gora* dramatises the built-in conflict in the dialectal relationship between the reformist and the revivalist movements. However, Tagore steers clear of the extremism represented by the obscurantism of the Hindus and the sectarianism of the Brahmos thereby dealing out an "even-handed justice"[15] to both these ill-conceived forces.

Gora—the foundling child of an Irish-English couple murdered in the Indian Sepoy Mutiny—is portrayed as the passionate advocate of Hindu revivalist nationalism. Though Gora's identity is hidden from him till the very end, it is revealed to the reader at the very beginning of the novel. Hence, the quality of irony gets built into the narrative, right at the start, thus presenting an ironic perspective in which the protagonist's mistaken identity and the resultant confusions and embarrassments define the very absurdity of the premises on which the purity of Hinduism is sought to be asserted. It is evident that Tagore got the idea for the novel from his meeting with sister Nivedita, formerly Margaret Noble who was a fervent disciple of Swami Vivekananda. In this regard, Krishna Kripalani remarks:

> Those who have read her books knew what a passionate advocate she was of everything Hindu. Tagore who liked and admired her for her sincerity and courage must often have smiled when she preached Hinduism to him—more Hindu than the Hindu: Once when she was staying as his guest at his Shelidah estate, she would insist, when they sat out on the deck of the house-boat in the evening, that he tell her a story. So he began telling the story of Gora and later wrote it down.[16]

The name "Gora" serves as a metaphor for the dubieties, anomalies and ironies, stemming from the ambiguity of his identity. It is conceived ironically for it means "white" which symbolises purity and light and is given to one, who, in orthodox Hindu terms, would be deemed most impure as a European mleccha. Gora's growth is depicted through a deepening perspective which highlights his growing uneasiness about his life's mission to revive Hindu society in its pristine purity, culminating in the revelation of his true identity, which, with the impact of a shattering seizure, affords him a knowledge of his hitherto blundering consciousness, naive idealism and blind faith. In his early years Gora symbolises the fate of an individual or society that becomes a prey to obscurantism and fanaticism, obfuscating whatever chances there are of finding a true direction in life.

The main plot of the novel concerns with Gora's attitudes, beliefs and conceptions and with his attempts at upholding them against disillusioning experiences and the final discovery of truth about himself whereas the Binoy-Lolita sub-plot brings into focus the Hindu-Brahmo conflicts. The main incidents of the plot serve as landmarks in the protagonist's journey of self-discovery. Early in the narrative, we are provided with insights into Gora's nature that he is addicted to extremisms, never doing anything half-heartedly. As "the acknowledged leader of a band of little revolutionaries," he always felt "too delighted if he got a chance in the street of quarrelling with an Englishman."[17] Later, as an enthusiast of the Brahmo Samaj, he was in the habit of harrying the Brahmin Pundits who gathered round his father whose newly cultivated orthodoxy prompts him to nearly cut off all relations with Gora. The Brahmin baiter is transformed, at the beginning of the story, into a Brahmo baiter by the learned pundit Vidyavagish and Gora plunges headlong into a fervent defence of "the blameless excellence of Hindu religion and society" (23) it is significant that in his writings and debates, he ends up, as the text records "....by succumbing to his own advocacy" (23). Thus, it is possible to detect a certain ambiguity—though he himself is not aware of it—about his stand which obviously concerns more with the ceremonial purity to be observed than with the realisation of inner purity, enjoined by the scriptures.

With a strong pollution complex Gora becomes most punctilious about ritual, bathing regularly in the Ganges, performing ceremonial worship in the morning and evening and taking particular care of what he touches and eats. He stops even taking water in his mother's room, as she keeps a Christian maid and does not also permit his friend and fellow crusader Binoy, to eat in her room. In dress, he becomes "....an incarnate image of revolt against modernity" (138), with a "tiki," coarse dhoti, and a castemark of Ganges clay. Taunting him his brother Mohim says:

> Many a bigot have I seen in my day, but this beats them all. You are going one better than even the Benares or Nadia pandits (64).

Tagore's nationalism is seen in Gora's opinion that foreign and native criticism of Hinduism can best be rebutted by holding firmly to our own customs and beliefs. He strongly opines:

> ....We must not feel apologetic about the country of our birth—whether it be about its traditions, faith, or its scriptures neither to others nor even to ourselves. We must save our country and ourselves from insult by manfully bearing the burden of our motherland with all our strength and all our pride (23).

When Hinduism is in the beleaguered state, he considers it his mission to defend casteism, rituals and superstitions to the point of being an unthinking fundamentalist. He proclaims to Binoy:

> ...Gourmohan is such an incorrigible fellow that he never apologises for his superstitions to any one at all (53).

By preparing that ground, as it were, Tagore now introduces the first of the many incidents that shake the self-complacency of this incorrigible neo-Hindu nationalist and sets him on the path of self-introspection.

As Gora cannot dissuade Binoy from visiting the Brahmo Samajists who are regarded as renegades, he himself pays a visit to the house of Paresh Babu where he stoutly defends Hindu rituals and rather rudely declines their hospitality. Despite his dislike for them, he cannot but be touched by Paresh Babu's saintliness and his foster daughter, Sucharita's tender beauty and keen intelligence. A strange restlessness overtakes Gora—partly due to the widening gulf between him and Binoy and partly due to the impact of his visits to Paresh Babu's family—

to escape which he undertakes a rural jaunt that turns out ultimately to be a journey into his innerself itself.

The novelist vividly records how Gora sees for himself the manner Hindu religion with its innumerable proscriptions and restrictions has kept the people divided and ignorant in the following words:

> ....to Gora it was a constant agony to be brought face to face with this terrible load of ignorance, apathy and suffering, which had overwhelmed rich and poor, learned and ignorant alike, and clogged their advance at every step (133).

Gora becomes aware that Hinduism, reduced in popular practice to "Prohibition, prohibition, nothing but prohibition" (164), has proved more a hindrance than a help for national regeneration. The novelist records:

> .....He could see nowhere any trace of that religion which through service, love, compassion, self-respect and respect for humanity as a whole gives power and life and happiness to all. The tradition which merely divided men into classes and separated class from class, driving to a distance love itself, did not want to carry into effect the results of man's intelligent thinking, and only put obstacles at every step in the way of man's coming and going. In these villages the cruel and evil results of this blind bondage were so clearly seen by Gora in all kinds of ways..., that was no longer possible for him to delude himself by the web of delusion which his own mind had woven (386).

Gora becomes aware of the futility of the strict observance of orthodox customs by Hindus without feelings of compassion for others in the predominantly Muslim village of Ghousepura whose natives had been fighting unitedly and daringly against the exploitation of foreign indigo planters, braving all tyranny and oppression by the police. The only Hindu resident of the village, a barber, had given shelter to a Muslim boy whose father had been imprisoned. Responding to Gora's reproach for his un-Hindu conduct, the barber says:

> What is the difference, Sir ? We call him as Hari, they as Allah, that's all (133).

Gora is moved by the contrast between the simple humanity of the unorthodox Hindu barber and the ignoble and selfish conduct of the Brahmin rent-collector of the Indigo factory—"A regular limb of Satan"(135). So he rejects the collector's hospitality and, going back to the barber's house, reflects:

> What terrible wrong have we been doing by making purity an external thing! Shall my caste remain pure by eating from the hands of this oppressor of the poor Mohemmedans and be lost in the home of the man who has not only shared their miseries but given shelter to one of them at the risk of being outcasted himself ? (136).

Thus time and again Gora is confronted with the shortcomings of Hinduism, but nevertheless holds on militantly to it through a mistaken notion of patriotism. When he does not succeed in either preventing Binoy's marriage to the Brahmo girl Lolita or persuading his mother against aiding him, Gora affirms his own commitment to his marriage:

> ...when the whole world has forsaken India and heaps insults upon her, I for my part which to share her seat of dishonour this caste-ridden, this superstitious, this idolatrous, India of mine! (267).

The above affirmation shows that Gora's intransigence springs from his resolve, come what may, to stand by his country, right or wrong. Any sort of staggering crisis cannot swerve him from his dogmatic stance. This comes about in the climactic scene when Gora stands exposed, with the hitherto-hidden secret of his birth now revealed to him, as one with "no mother, no father, no country, no nationality, no lineage, no God even" (402). As Bhabani Bhattacharya observes, Gora has absorbed the shock of the revelation, because he had been yearning for an escape from "the inner strains of his self-imposed obligations."[18] If his intellectual dogmatism blinds him for a time, his emotional resilience comes into play after his release from gaol. Earlier, because of his punctilious orthodoxy, he had kept women away from his field of vision and was totally opposed to their appearance in public and participation in national life. During his incarceration, he is haunted by the image of Sucharita, and when he meets her after his release, he begins to reflect about the problem. The novelist remarks:

> Gora was astonished at his own thoughts. He had never realised before how imperfect his perception of India had been as long as he had failed to acknowledge the women of India. What a lack there had been in Gora's perception of his duty to his country as long as its women were so shadowy and unreal to him ! It was as though his idea of duty had power but no life, muscles but no nerves. Gora realised in a single moment that the further we banish woman from us, and the smaller the place we give to her in our lives, the weaker does our manhood become (273).

Freed from all bonds, Gora projects himself as the true Indian whom neither caste nor race nor nationality can inhibit. He proclaims:

> ....Today I am really an Indian ! In me there is no longer any opposition between Hindu, Mussalman and Christian. Today every caste in India is my caste, the food of all is my food! .....all these days I have been carrying about with me an unseen gulf of separation which I have never been able to cross over ! Therefore, in my mind there was a kind of void, which I tried by various devices to ignore. I tried to make that emptiness look more beautiful by decorating it with all kinds of artistic work. Because I loved India better than life itself I was quite unable to bear the least criticism of that part of it which I had got to know. Now that I have been delivered from those fruitless attempts at inventing such useless decorations I feel, Paresh Babu, that I am alive again! (406).

Various critics have criticised the way the denouement has been brought about. B.C. Chakravorty takes it as "an artificial solution"[19] while Nirad C. Chaudhuri opines that " ...a victory for liberal cosmopolitanism is pulled off only by means of a *deux ex machina*."[20] Sujit Mukherjee regards it "the most serious weakness of the novel"[21] and S.C. Sengupta comments it as:

> If Gora had been able to resolve the contradiction through a spiritual struggle, his story would have made a great novel. But Rabindranath betrays here an indolence about fundamentals; rather than portray the intricate spiritual struggle that is aroused in Gora's heart, he ends it mechanically almost as soon as it begins.[22]

But G.V. Raj opines "that these critics have not paid adequate attention to the subtle changes of Gora's consciousness traced in the novel."[23] A close perusal of the text indicates that the freeing process commences the moment Gora steps into the home of Paresh Babu right at the start of the novel, soon after which he is seized with a new restlessness, brought about by "...the memory of the questioning glances of two entrancing eyes, soft with modesty, bright with understanding..." (107). The conflict between his intellectual dogmatism and emotional resilience thus begins early, though outwardly Gora does not betray signs of it. Even his rigid stance on ceremonial purity has behind it a strategic intention, since Gora believes that offence is the best form of defence. To Sucharita's question about Gora's "touch-me-notism," Binoy replies:

> "....I know quite well that is merely his dogmatism,—the more absurd his opinions sound to his hearers, the more positively will he express them. He insists on rigid, indiscriminate observance, lest, by his yielding on minor points, foolish people may be led to feel a disrespect for more vital matters, or lest the opposite party should claim a victory. So he dare not display any laxity even to me" (88).

The excellence of Tagore's artistry lies in his reserving the revelation of Gora's identity to a moment when he is about to be proclaimed as "The Light of Hinduism." If accomplished, it could have been an inversion of his inward process of revaluation, which underlies the plot structure of the novel. Having detailed Gora's muffled voices from within about the incalculable damage done to Hindu society by the prevalence of superstition and obscurantism, Tagore clinches the insights with the final discovery of his identity. Hence, the final denouement is not in the nature of a *deux ex machina* but of a *coup de grace* device.

Towards the end of the novel Gora realises the ideal of liberal cosmopolitanism. This is already exemplified in the roles of Paresh Babu and Anandamoyi who also face a crisis of identity, though of a different nature. Both find themselves out of their element in their societies because of their complete freedom from bigotry and sectarianism. As an upholder of the Brahmo Samaj traditions, Paresh Babu becomes the target of sectarian attacks from his own group, now dominated by the likes of Haran Babu, and Baroda Sundari. His wide tolerance and firm faith in the oneness of all religions never waver:

> ....The bigots are those whose idea is, Truth depends me, I do not depend Truth. As for myself, I pray to God that I may always be a simple worshipper of truth, whether in a Brahmo temple or at a Hindu shrine—that no external barrier may obstruct or hinder my worship (89).

Paresh Babu is projected as an embodiment of a non-sectarian, all embracing religious outlook and not surprisingly Gora is made at the end to turn to him with these words:

> It is you who have the mantram of that freedom and that is why today you find no place in any society. Make me your disciple. Today give me the mantram of that Deity who belongs to all, Hindu, Mussalman, Christian, and Brahmo alike—the doors to whose temple are never closed to any person of any caste whatever—He who is

> not merely the god of the Hindus, but who is the God of India herself (407)!

Anandamoyi, one of Tagore's noblest creations, emerges from the novel as the eternal type of Indian mother, who in her tender loving care, is not inhibited by caste, creed or nationality.

Liberated from the darkness of soul which had held him in thrall for so long, Gora extols her as the very epitome of Indian spirit:

> ....The mother whom I have been wondering about in search of was all the time sitting in my room at home. You have no caste, you make no distinctions, and have no hatred—you are only the image of our welfare! It is you who are India! (407).

Anandamoyi, the daughter of a learned Benares scholar, discards "the traditions of seven generations" (13) and chooses to be an outcast in her own house for her love of Gora whom being childless, she regards as a god's gift to her. Without succumbing to the blandishments of Gora, she assumes the responsibility for Binoy's marriage to Lolita which is objected to by the rigidly sectarian Brahmos as well. Her defence of the marriage gives an indication of her enlightened mind, free from all vestiges of communal bigotry and religious intolerance:

> ...Marriage is a matter of hearts coming together—if that happens, what matters it what mantras are recited? ....There is no caste in men's hearts—there God brings men together and there He Himself comes to them. Will it ever do to keep Him at a distance and leave the duty of uniting men to creeds and forms? (183).

Both Paresh Babu and Anandamoyi, as idealised characters, "stand isolated in their respective families and exemplify the ideals which Gora comes to cherish towards the end of the novel, the distinction between the two being that the former has gained a breadth of vision by his intellect and the latter through the warmth of her heart."[24]

Sucharita, Lolita and Binoy are portrayed by Tagore to bring into focus the Hindu-Brahmo conflict, which forms the secondary theme of the novel. Radharani, whose Hindu name is changed to Sucharita when she is adopted by Paresh Babu, becomes engaged to the Brahmo zealot, Haran Babu. But because of Haran Babu's sectarianism and intolerance she is progressively alienated from him and feels drawn to Gora, despite Gora's rigid Hindu orthodoxy because his burning patriotism finds a sympathetic echo in her. The arrival of her Hindu aunt, Harimohini whom she has to take care of, creates more problems for her with Paresh Babu's wife who cannot countenance an idol-worshipper in her house. Though deeply attached to Paresh Babu, Sucharita is compelled by circumstances to leave him. But the deep spiritual non-sectarian outlook she has imbibed from him helps to rise above narrow prejudices and take her side by Gora after his redemption from his xenophobic obscurantism.

The deep antagonism and division between the Hindu and Brahmo sects, represented by Gora on the one side and Baroda Sundari and Haran Babu on the other have been brought to the surface by the Binoy-Lolita episode. Each group opposes their marriage or insists on the marriage being performed according to their own ritual. Commenting on the uncompromising stand of the two sects, Paresh Babu says:

> What to Him is the Brahmo Samaj! What is Hindu Society: He sees only Man (309).

However, with the assistance of Anandamoyi, Binoy and Lolita are united. Later, their union, like that of Gora and Sucharita, symbolises the path of unity between the two divergent faiths (Hindu and Brahmo).

The presentation of a fair amount of debate forming the major body of the novel, is a significant feature of the novel. About the textual composition of the novel Niharranjan Ray remarks that Tagore had taken a large extracts from his essays and lectures and incorporated them in *Gora* in the form of conversations and discussions.[25] So the novel is an embodiment of Tagore's integrated vision of a syncretistic India which finds poetic expression in the following lines:

> Come ye Aryan, come non-Aryan, Hindu, Muslim, come, come ye English, come ye Christians, welcome everyone, come Brahmin, cleanse your mind and clasp the hand of all, come ye outcaste, come ye lowly, fling away the load of shame!
>
> Come one and all, to the Mother's Crowning, the sacred jar is yet to fill, and all must join that the water be consecrate on the shore of this vast sea of humanity that is India.[26]

Commenting on the quality of the novel K.R. Srinivasa Iyengar says:

> "Notwithstanding the wide canvas and the multiplicity of character, incident and dialogue, the novel is a unity—and this comes from Gora himself, who is both centre and circumference. The rest serve largely to explain him, or arc explained by his relations with them."[27]

In this novel Gora's character has been depicted with wider catholicity and sympathy. He is shown as a symbol of the rising nationalism of the early twentieth century in India. He represents the aspirations and sentiments of the educated Bengalis of his age, who agitated against the injustice and arrogance of the British rulers, and being conscious of their slavery, tried to seek out their cultural heritage and protect it from all types of onslaughts. To Gora, therefore, everything that is Indian is sacred and everything that is Indian is to be interpreted in terms of undiluted Hinduism. By giving emphasis on the cultural unity of India transcending caste, sect and religion, Tagore not only asserts the value of humanism in life but also points out the dangers faced by the national awakening in the country at the beginning of the twentieth century. He warns his countrymen against the drifting of the national movement towards a militant Hinduism under the stormy influence of extremist leaders like Tilak, Bipinchandra Pal, and Aurobindo Ghosh. "Besides, by depicting the ironical situation of a white man cultivating the unbounded love for Hindu religion and nation, the author appears to suggest that religion and patriotism are not ingrained in the blood of a man from birth but are contacted by him from his surroundings and environments."[28]

Summing up, *Gora* can be viewed in the nationalist perspective through Gora's conscious effort to exalt Hinduism and build Indian nationalism on its basis.

(VIII) *THE HOME AND THE WORLD*

Tagore's novel *The Home and the World* deals with two themes, the Swadeshi Movement in Bengal (1903-08) and the extra marital love affair. The former theme forms the backdrop for the story wherein Tagore depicts how unscrupulous politicians, by their glib talk on patriotism, mislead the people to satisfy their greed and lust. While the first theme has political overtones, the second exposes the murky morality of high society. Through this "Rabindranath threw a veritable bombshell on the conservative society"[29] and it created such a shattering impact that for "three long years after its publication the critics continued to tear the novel to pieces."[30] On the basis of the first theme the novel may be viewed in the nationalist perspective.

Depicting the Swadeshi Movement in Bengal along with the portrayal of an impressionable, young housewifes' traumatic passage into the world outside the home and back, the novel carries the spirit of nationalism and humanism. Set against the stormy days of the revolutionary background of 1905 Bengal chocked with the war cries of "Swadeshi" and "Bandemataram," the novel depicts the autobiographical sketches of three principal characters—Nikhil, his wife Bimala and Sandip, his friend. Bimala, who has lived sheltered life of a Hindu wife, suddenly hears the call of the outside world and thus she is torn between the pull of the "home" and the pull of "world." Here Tagore points out how "love could come in conflict more narrowly, more fiercely with politics also."[31] He narrates the poignant story of a woman undergoing a terrible mental tension and turmoil by taking part in the Swadeshi Movement and being torn asunder by the conflicting loyalties to the house and the outside world. In this simple story of a love triangle, he makes Nikhil and Sandip represent the conflict between idealism and realism, or truth and illusion. In fact, this novel is strongly ideological because of the implications of the critical debate between Gandhism and terrorist politics.

In this novel Tagore portrays the conflict between nationalism and universal manhood vividly and gives the most profound expression to his faith in the perfect independence and freedom for an individual irrespective of any particular nationality. He makes Sandip represent the pugnacious natioanalism and narrow-minded patriotism of the politically conscious Indians during the Swadeshi Movement. Sandip is as typical Machiavellian patriot who exhorts the people recklessly to burn British goods and resort to violence when opposed.

In fact, the novel unfolds the trials and tribulations of a home, caught up in the convulsions of a political struggle, with profound implications for the individual and the nation alike. The action of the novel is predicated on two movements—one, an inward movement towards the projection of the home as a world in miniature and the other, an outward movement towards the perspectivisation of the world as a larger home, a greater home as it were. The novel seeks to define the inter-relatedness between the home and the world, between family life and life outside with a view to emphasising the dangers of the outside world to immature and impetuous minds. In a review of the novel E.M. Forster has commented that "He (Tagore) meant the wife to be seduced by the world, which is, with all its sins, a tremendous lover; she is actually seduced by a West Kesington Babu..." and also underrated the novel as "a boarding-house flirtation that masks itself in mystic or patriotic talk."[32] This flawed perception of the Indian society in the turbulent Swadeshi Movement days makes Forster interpret Tagore on the superficial plane and lose sight of the dialectical interplay of the essential values symbolised in the novel under the stress of the upheaval.

The novel raises problems of profound significance: the meaning of true patriotism, the correlation of ends and means in any struggle for human emancipation, the pulls and counterpulls of home and the world in women's consciousness and the perils inherent in their attempts at apprehending the truth of their very being. In his examination of these issues Tagore persuasively argues in favour of the essential human values of love, loyalty, and truth in both the private and the public spheres of contemporary Indian life. It is through a reconciliation of home with the world with their symbolic connotations that one could hope for self-fulfilment. Love and loyalty which sustain the home are not incompatible with love and loyalty to the country. There is no need to break the one in order to build the other. The novel's distinction lies in identifying the outer world of political strife and the internal world of domestic tension with the quest for a creative equilibrium between the two.

The novel's dominant theme is the triangular relationship involving Nikhil, Bimala and Sandip. The Swadeshi Movement activates and complicates this relationship highlighting the tension and conflict between the home and the world. Starting as a broadbased and united protest against the partition of Bengal (1905), the Movement was conceived, as the expression "Swadeshi" actively supported the Movement by starting a Swadeshi Bhandar in Calcutta for the promotion of indigenous goods as early as 1897 and by composing a number of national song, leading processions and raising funds for funding National Schools. But he withdrew from it when the Swadeshi Movement assumed the form of a mere political agitation producing extreme reactions. From the serene surroundings of Santiniketan, he watched with anguish the havoc being wrought by intemperate nationalism: the burning of much-needed cloth in the name of boycott of foreign goods and the alienating of Muslims by introducing Hindu religious motifs in the struggle.

Tagore explained the reasons for his withdrawal from the Swadeshi agitation which appeared to him to have degenerated into a negative campaign of hatred and exclusiveness, in one of his letters to C.F. Andrews, as: "the anarchy of emptiness never tempts me, even when it is resorted to as temporary measure."[33] So, in a sense, *The Home and the World* may be regarded as Tagore's assessment of the Movement in fictional form. As Samit Sarkar, one of the historians of the Movement writes:

> ...the complexities of the Swadeshi Age—its grandeur and its pettiness, its triumphs and problems and tragedies—have indeed been immortalised in the writings of the greatest literary figure of the times."[34]

Though the novel records faithfully certain aspects of the political struggle in Bengal, it transcends the purely historical situation and acquires a larger significance, as Niharranjan Ray observes in the following words:

> ...because of its vivid and ironic indictment of unscrupulous politicians, of its denunciation of violence, aggressive intents and methods, and chauvinistic nationalism, and of the humanist logic of good ends being the product of good means, and equally humanist ideals of love and truth and any given situation.[35]

Though the novel evolved much interest abroad because of the relevance of its perspectives to situations in other countries as well, it is not an investigation of the Swadeshi Movement *in toto* but only a dramatisation of its implications for individuals and their relations with one another in the hectic days of the struggle. As Bhabani Bhattacharya writes :

> ...it is the human interest in *The Home and the World* that mainly counts. The characters are no pawns in the hands of history, even if they are good symbols.[36]

Nikhil and Sandip, the two male protagonists, exemplify the parameters of approach to the problem of Indian emancipation, the former's a rationalistic, constructive approach with emphasis on self-reliance and righteous means, and the latter's that of emotional extremism, questionable means, crude nationalism, and brute force. Tagore's own vision of the struggle for independence seems to be reflected in Nikhil's concept of freedom, self-government, and constructive leadership. Like Nikhil in the novel, Tagore had to face unpopularity, isolation and even hostility due to his apposition to coercive and frenzied patriotism. As Krishna Kripalani observes:

> Not even in his fiercest outburst of patriotism would Tagore be jingoistic which may partly explain why among his own people he was never popular, whatever the praises sung after his death.[37]

Long before the advent of the Swadeshi Movement, Nikhil, a patriot to the core, had done his best to encourage indigenous manufacture in his estates, though without much success. A rich Zamindar, he could afford the luxury of imported goods but preferred native ones. When the boycott of foreign goods had become a fashionable slogan, his wife Bimala recounts:

> ....And yet, some time ago, when my husband began to import country-made articles into our village, he had been secretly and openly twitted for his folly, by old and young alike. When Swadeshi had not yet become a boast, we had despised it with all our hearts.[38]

Contrary to Nikhil's genuine patriotism, Sandip's is opportunistic and a means for achieving personal power. He is, in fact the prototype of a "populist" demagogue—hypocritical and unscrupulous, capable of sweeping along everyone with his magnetism, sophistry, and rhetoric. His braggadocio is illustrated by the passage from his diary as given below:

> Am I not born to rule? to bestride my proper steed, the crowd and drive it as I will, the reins in my hand, the destination known only to me, and for it the thorns, the

> mire, on the road ? This steed now awaits me at the door, pawing and champing its bit, its neighing filling the skies (103).

Sandip is not only inculcating the Swadeshi spirit among the people but also inflaming them with the cult of Bande Mataram and the concept of freedom by force. Through this game of Sandip Nikhil sees the kind of man "...who needs must shout and deify their country in order to keep up their excitement,—these love excitement more than their country" (45), but also realises that his restraint and moral stance would have no appeal to the mass mind. He, nevertheless, does not flinch from his stand however unpopular it is and so he remarks:

> I am willing to serve my country; but my worship I reserve for Right which is far greater than my country. To worship my country as a god is to bring a curse upon it (26).

He further declares:

> So long as we are impervious to truth and have to be moved by some hypnotic stimulus, we must know that we lack the capacity for self-government (45).

Thus the main conflict of the novel is based on the antithetical postures of the two friends—Nikhil and Sandip.

Anchored in the love of her husband, the modern-minded Nikhil, who arranges for her English education and introduces her to modern ways of life Bimala has led a happy married life for nine years. Nikhil longs to find her blossom fully in the knowledge of herself in the wide world outside. So he urges her to step into it by saying:

> What I want is, that I should have you and you should have me more fully in the outside world, ...I would have you come into the heart of the outer world and meet reality.... If we meet and recognise each other, in the real world, then only will our love be true (18).

But she declines to come out of the Zenana as she keeps regard for the conventions of the Rajah's house where she is perfectly content with her life. Recalling this life she remarks:

> I have read in books that we are called "caged birds." I cannot speak for others, but I had so much in this cage of mine that there was not room for it in the universe,—at least that is what I then felt (19).

The impact of the eruption of the Swadeshi Movement is felt even in the innermost recesses of every home in Bengal. It also breaks down the barriers between the home and the world for Bimala. She recounts the situation as:

> One day there came the new era of Swadeshi in Bengal: but as to how it happened we have no distinct vision. There was no gradual slope connecting the past with the present. For that reason, I imagine, the new epoch came like a flood, breaking down the dykes and sweeping all our prudence and fear before it. We had no time even to think about, or understand, what had happened, or what was about to happen.
>
> My sight and my mind, my hopes and my desires, became red with the passion of this news age. Though, up to this time, the walls of the home—which was the ultimate world to my mind—remained unbroken, yet I stood looking over into the distance, and I heard a voice from the far horizon, whose meaning was not perfectly clear to me, but whose call went straight to my heart (22-23).

Bimala has the eagerness to do some personal sacrifice and so she wants to get rid of her English teacher, Miss Gilby and also burn her foreign clothes but is dissuaded by her husband who suggests her thus:

> ....why this bonfire business? ....
>
> Why not try to build up some thing?
>
> You should not waste even a tenth part of your energies in this destructive excitement (24).

Bimala feels unhappy because her husband simply supports Swadeshi, but not whole-heartedly adopts the spirit of *Bande Mataram*. Unbeknown to herself, she has a longing for the flamboyant and passionate, and hence, her husband's "dull, milk-and-watery Swadeshi" (122) does not appeal to her.

At this critical juncture in the story Tagore tactfully introduces Sandip whose fiery eloquence holds Bimala spellbound. In the meeting where Sandip delivers his speech, sitting behind a screen, Bimala listens and she impatiently pushes it away—the action is symbolical that now she is face to face with the world—fixes her gaze upon him. Later she records:

> I was no longer the lady of the Raja's house, but the sole representative of Bengal's womanhood. And he was the champion of Bengal.... I said within myself that his language had caught fire from my eyes; for we women are not only the deities of the household fire, but the flame of the soul itself (28-29).

The unscrupulous Sandip cleverly exploits Bimala's delusions of being the "Sakti of the Motherland" by laying a snare for her mind and body through clever flattery. On the pretext of promoting Swadeshi, he stays on with Nikhil and pursues his strategy of seduction of Bimala by extolling her as the "Queen Bee" of the Swadeshi workers. When she is told that all the country is in need of her, Bimala feels exalted. She utters:

> Sandip's hungry eyes burnt like the lamps of worship before my shrine. All his gaze proclaimed that I was a wonder in beauty and power; and the loudness of his praise, spoken and unspoken, drowned all other voices in my world. Had the Creator created me afresh, I wondered? Did he wish to make up now for neglecting me so long? I who before was plain had become suddenly beautiful. I who before had been of no account now felt in myself all the splendour of Bengal itself (56-57).

Though perturbed and pained by Bimala's growing infatuation with Sandip, Nikhil decides not to intervene but to wait patiently for her to realise the truth of circumstance and recant herself from her headlong rush to ruin. He can easily expose Sandip for the hypocrite that he is—his habit of glorifying his selfish lusts under high sounding names—but desists from doing so for the following reasons:

> It will, however, be difficult to explain to Bimala today that Sandip's love of country is but a phase of his covetous self-love. Bimala's hero-worship of Sandip makes me hesitate all the more to talk to her about him, lest some touch of jealousy may lead me unwittingly into exaggeration (46-47).

Nikhil's idealised image of Bimala has to reckon with the stubborn reality of her nature—her partiality for the audacious, the tumultous in men and he feels that it is upto her to realise her error. If she cannot liberate herself from her delusions, he would rather bow out of her life than exercise the traditional authority of a husband over a wife to claim her back. To quote Nikhil:

> I must not lose my faith: I shall wait. The passage from the narrow to the larger world is stormy. When she is familiar with this freedom, then I shall know where my place is. If I discover that I do not fit in with the arrangements of the outer world, then I shall not quarrel with my fate, but silently take my leave.... Use force? But for what ? Can force prevail against Truth? (49).

Sandip has forgotten the patriotic cause which has drawn Bimala to him; his conversation takes an intimate, personal turn. Bimala is not altogether unaware of Sandip's designs; yet she feels hypnotised by him, unable to free herself from his spell. She confesses thus:

> I will not shirk the truth. This cataclysmal desire drew me by day and by night. It seemed desperately alluring,—thus making havoc of myself. What a shame it seemed,

> how terrible and yet how sweet? Then there was my overpowering curiosity to which there seemed no limit. He of whom I knew but little, who never could assuredly be mine, whose youth flared so vigorously in a hundred points of flame—oh, the mystery of his seething passions, so immense, so tumultous! (83).

It is Sandip's passionate rhetoric that enthrals Bimala. It is evident from what she reminisces as:

> Sandip's eyes took fire as he went on, but whether it was the fire of worship, or of passion, I could not tell. I was reminded of the day on which I first heard him speak, when I could not be sure whether he was a person, or just a living flame (91).

Her husband's refusal to banish foreign goods from the markets in his estates provokes Sandip and his followers to resort to violence. Nikhil's argument is that it is upto the people to choose between indigenous and foreign goods. He declares: "To tyrannise for the country is to tyrannise over the country" (142). As the Muslim traders are particularly obdurate, Sandip's followers sink a boat, and as its owner, one Mirjan, threatens to go to the police, it becomes necessary to pay him some hush money. As usual in his flamboyant manner, Sandip asks Bimala for a sum of fifty thousand, but settles for five thousand at the end. Bimala steals the sovereigns of gold from her own home and the indignity of it sets her on the path of self-introspection:

> The burden of the theft crushed my heart to the dust.... I could not think of my home as separate from my country; I had robbed my house, I had robbed my country. For this sin my house has ceased to be mine, my country also was estranged from me (192-93).

The turning point in the story occurs when she goes to present the gold sovereigns to Sandip. Seeing all that gold, Sandip is unable to restrain himself and springs forward as if to embrace Bimala in congratulation; she thrusts him away from her—a symbolical release for her. He reels back from hitting his head on the edge of a marble table and drops to the floor. Bimala recounts thus:

> The moment I had stolen my husband's money and paid it to Sandip, the music that was in our relations stopped. Not only did I destroy all my own value by making myself cheap, but Sandip's powers, too, lost scope for their full play.... Sandip has lost his aspect of the hero; a tone of low quarrelsomeness has come into his words (211).

Sandip betrays his covetousness and jealousy when Bimala hands over her jewels to Amulya, the young revolutionary, to be sold to replace the stolen amount. She now sees him in his true colours and realises that all his eloquence is mere bluster and all his songs of praise false. She exclaims:

> Sandip, the wielder of magic spells, is reduced to utter powerlessness, whenever his spell refuses to work. From a king he fell to the level of a boor.... His snaky coils, with which he used to snare me, are exhausted, I am free. I am saved, saved (240).

Ultimately Bimala is restored to Nikhil and receives his blessing but she cannot get rid of the feeling that her disastrous journey into the world has left its permanent marks on her. She remarks:

> ....What keeps crushing my heart is the thought that the festive flutes which were played at my wedding nine years ago, welcoming me to this house, will never sound for me again in his life.... How many years, how many ages, aeons, must pass before I can find my way back to that day of nine years ago? (255).

However, Bimala's reunion with Nikhil does not last long. Sandip's attempts to turn nation-worship into Kali-worship and his joining forces with a neighbouring Zamindar in coercing Muslim tenants to take to Swadeshi, result in a break out of communal riots and Nikhil rushes out in defence of the women of the neighbouring Zamindar's house and is seriously hurt. The novel ends with Bimala disconsolately gazing out the distant flames as Nikhil is brought in a palanquin with serious head injuries followed by a litter of Amulya Babu who is "done for," with a bullet in his heart.

Learned critics have variously interpreted *The Home and the World* as "a defence of certain principles but also, in a way, the author's defence of his own role,"[39] that is in the Swadeshi Movement, "a devastating exposure of those black-hearted 'Patriots' who shut the door on truth and humanity and right, and for their own utterly selfish ends inflamed immature minds to frenzy in the name of patriotism,"[40] "the best picture of Bengal's time of political awakening,"[41] "an allegorical tale with Bimala representing India, Nikhil all that is good and vital in the Indian tradition and Sandip personifying the aggressive, western-type nationalism,"[42] and "a psychological study of relationship between a husband and his wife."[43]

With some truth in all these observations, the novel can also be interpreted as "primarily a delineation of the delusions and discoveries of self of the principal characters—Bimala's delusions of grandeur, about herself and about Sandip, Nikhil's delusions of Bimala and Sandip's delusions of Bimala and himself which are powerfully dramatised in their interaction to the objective reality—the Swadeshi Movement against alien rule."[44] The interplay of delusions and discoveries gains in psychological intensity by Tagore's adept use of the multiple points of view technique which makes for a clearer enunciation of the motives and states of mind of the principal character. The device of presenting separate segments of the story through different characters helps Tagore to highlight the internal conflicts and convulsions, leading to the discovery of self in the central character of Bimala. In fact, "Bimala is able to realise the explosive potentialities of a self-centred Sandip who under the guise of a chauvinistic stance unscrupulously exploits the religious and patriotic sentiments of the people with disastrous results almost breaking Bimala's home life by postulating a false connection between the home and the world."[45]

In this novel, Tagore, with a prophetic vision, anticipates the method Indians were to employ in their struggle for independence. He seems to suggest that for sometime India may, like Bimala, be hypnotised by the violent forces but ultimately it will resort to non-violent methods advocated by Nikhil. The novel raises certain fundamental social and political issues like the role of women at home and outside, the equality of the sexes and the relation between the Hindus and Muslims in a pluralistic society like ours. Krishna Kripalani comments that "the novel is equally a testament of Gandhi's philosophy of non-violence, love and truth, of his insistent warning that evil means must vitiate the end, however nobly conceived."[46] Dr. Sukumar Sen also comments that "in this novel Tagore draws the contrast between the old ways and the new at home and outside."[47]

To sum up, the novelist, through Bimala's character, records the transition of ladies from their secluded life in the Zenana to the national politics by taking part in the National Movement.

(IX) *FOUR CHAPTERS*

Rabindranath Tagore's last novel, *Four Chapters* written in Ceylon in 1934 raised a cloud of protest and controversy since the background of the story is "vividly coloured by the passions aroused by the political struggle and turmoil in modern Bengal."[48] Sisirkumar Ghose comments that "it dealt with the extremist or underground activities which had never appealed to Tagore."[49] Humayun Kabir rightfully comments that "*Four Chapters* deals with the revolutionary movement which sought to achieve Indian independence through individual acts of terror."[50] In the same vein Dr. K.R.S. Iyengar also comments that "in *Four Chapters* the indictment of political fanaticism is as pointed and incisive as the glorification of human love is almost apocalyptic."[51] Here Tagore made clear his views on political terrorism and fanaticism.

Deeply hurt by the politician's glib talk on patriotism, he makes the hero Atindra tell the heroine Ela:

> The patriotism of those who have no faith in that which is above patriotism is like a crocodile's back used as a ferry to cross the river. Meanness, unfaithfulness, mutual mistrust, secret machination, plotting for leadership—sooner or later these drag them into the mud at the bottom. That the life of the country can be saved by killing its soul, is a monstrously false doctrine that nationalists all over the world are bellowing forth stridently, my heart groans to give it effective contradiction (63).

In spite of various protesting interpretations of the theme of the novel cited above and elsewhere, it may be viewed in the nationalist perspective also. Dr. Sukumar Sen rightly remarks:

> There is an attempt here to analyse the real motives and values of the revolutionary activities of violence in Bengal that followed the Non-Cooperation Movement.... Tagore's deep sympathy for the independence movement and his admiration for the young men and women who sacrificed themselves for the cause of independence, has found glowing expression in this last novel of his.[52]

The novel starts with a declaration of high political resolve but very soon hopeless love becomes its dominant theme.

In fact, in this novel Tagore deals with the theme of the tragic dialectic between political agitation and human values. So at the deeper level, the theme of the story is the love of Ela and Atindra. Here Tagore's primary concern is not with the political issues but with their impact on individual lives which acquire a psychological intensification on account of their being presented against the stormy background of revolutionary struggles. Any critical evaluation of the novel based on its historical framework alone would be inadequate. The nature and course of love between Ela and Atin—the principal characters—needs to be interpreted, however, in terms of not only their individual characters but also their interaction of self and circumstances.

Tagore stresses the importance of the exterior circumstances in moulding and testing a character and it is this interaction that is the seminal point of the story. Besides, many consider the book is an indictment against revolutionary violence. But to make the position clear Tagore himself states:

> What might be called the only theme of the book is the love of Ela and Atindra. The nature and course of the love between man and woman is determined not only by the individual characters of the lovers; it is influenced also by the impact of their circumstances on them. The river brings down its gushing nature from the mountain top that gives it birth, but it acquires its distinctiveness from the contour of the land through which it flows. The same is the case with love. On the one hand, there is the inner feeling, on the other, the conflict with outward circumstances. It is the combination of these two factors that gives the complete picture its individuality. I have tried in this story to body forth that individuality in the love of Ela and Atindra. I have had to show the capital asset of their natures, as well as to render an account of their transactions which the outside world with which they had to deal to the last (VI).... The revolutionary movement in Bengal has provided their love with its special dramatic setting. Descriptions of the movement are of secondary importance: what matters as literature is the portrayal of the poignance and pain of their love against the stormy background of the revolution (IX).

Tagore was convinced about the utter futility of the terrorist path for the attainment of the country's freedom. To quote Leonard A. Gordon:

> In the spring of 1908, after several murders and revolutionary "actions" had taken place, Tagore felt called upon to make his position known. He wrote two essays on the situation at the time entitled *Path O Prakreya* (The

> Way and the Means) and Samasya (The Problem).... He characterised the revolutionary acts in the same way that he described many other political activities in the Swadeshi period; they were all attempts at short cuts. "Just because I am in a hurry" wrote Tagore, "the road does not shorten." In a variety of expressions that an artist has at his command, Tagore described the revolutionaries and all exclusively political nationalists as sudden sparks, storms, people who wanted to fly instead of walk, and people taking a drink who might fall into the unfortunate situation of making the alcohol an end in itself. Their actions, those sudden spurt of energy, were not equal to the tasks confronting India. They were no substitute for the creative process and the sustained arduous work that was needed. Tagore's point was not that their action was an evil to be condemned without reflection, but that it was not the best way to achieve the goals on which all might agree.[53]

Tagore's warnings about the self-defeating nature of political terrorism, though unheeded at the time, came true later on. In this regard, Sasadhar Sinha remarks:

> The period of terrorism was an arid episode in Indian politics and its impact on Bengal in particular proved to be disastrous.... Hundreds of impressionable young Bengalis—men and women—were drawn into the terrorist movement, which meant that scores of families were totally ruined, many young men paying the penalty with their lives. Others wasted their youth in penal servitude or long periods of detention.....
>
> Their sacrifices were destined to come to nothing. They had realised their mistake but often alas, too late.[54]

Tagore, in the preface to the novel, describes at length how Brahmabandhav Upadhyay, a noted scholar and a boyhood friend of Swami Vivekananda, influenced the minds and hearts of Bengali youth during the Swadeshi Movement with his rhetoric of extremist nationalism, only to become disillusioned at the end. He writes:

> "On the one hand he was a Roman Catholic ascetic and on the other a Vedantist—fiery, fearless, unattached, widely known, immensely influential. I was drawn to him by profound respect for his extraordinary spiritual zeal and intellect....he was the first to join me as a colleague at the foundation of my educational institution at Santiniketan....
>
> At this juncture Lord Curzon had firmly resolved to partition Bengal. Hindu-Muslim discord, arising out of this decision, had already cast its blood-red shadow on the political scene.... Just then, this ascetic hurled himself into the vortex that has been stirred up by the countryside churning of the emotions. He himself brought out an evening paper *Sandhya*. The intoxicating wine that he had started pouring into it in vigorous language set the country's blood on fire.... I had not met him for a long time in this period.... Upadhyay appeared suddenly. He had by then been caught in the mesh of his Karma, there was no escaping it. This was my last meeting and talk with him.... It is perhaps worth recording this event at the opening of the novel."[55]

The descriptive vividness with which the seamy side of terrorism is evoked in the novel has provoked controversy. But as Tagore avers, such controversy "falls outside the province of literary criticism" (V). What the novel presents cannot be and should not be measured against the actual political situation in Bengal since it creates its own world in which the characters are products of circumstances under the plot structure of the novel. Hence, it cannot be said that it articulates any condemnation or praise concerning realities beyond the projections envisaged in it. As Srikumar Bannerjee states:

> There is a charge levelled against Rabindranath that he has not given a true picture of the revolutionary cult. If true, it is beside his purpose.... Rabindranath's poetic

> standard of values makes him choose the inherent weakness of terrorism as his main theme and not its outward strength.[56]

Tagore was deeply moved by the futile martyrdom of young, idealistic patriots at the altar of terrorism. He was convinced that the destructive potentialities of the cult of violence were greater than any political gains accruing from it. He dramatises the tragic impact of terrorism on human lives through the roles of Ela and Atin, particularly when there is an inbuilt flaw in revolutionary leadership as exemplified by Indranath.

Though the novel provides the perspectives on political terrorism, it cannot be termed a political novel since the main focus is on the course of love of Atin and Ela and the complications arising out of the conflict between love of man and woman and that of man and cause. Indeed, the main characters come to assume different postures of love in the course of the novel's action. Indranath exemplifies self-love of a most ignoble kind since it is his personal frustration rather than love of country that impels him to take to the terrorist path. He uses terrorism as an instrument of personal power to avenge his humiliation at the hands of the British Government which has thwarted his ambitions of scientific fame by depriving him of a career in research. While in Europe, he became a political suspect and found, on coming back home, that every door to advancement was closed to him. Through the special recommendation of an eminent English scientist, he secures the post of a teacher but is sent to a college without a laboratory. Seeing no prospect of recognition and honour in his career, he resigns and starts an institution for teaching French and German, which serves as a front for his revolutionary activity. He boasts to Kanai by saying:

> They tried to make me petty by closing the doors on every side. I'm determined to show them that I'm great, even if that entails disaster at every step. You can see for yourself, Kanai, how these followers have come round

> me at my call, recking nothing of life or death, Why? Because I know how to call. That's what I want to make clear to myself and others; and, after that, I don't care what happens (21-22).

In fact, Indranath has the necessary charisma and intellect coupled with ruthlessness to become the commander of the movement. Appreciating his quality Tagore writes:

> Some believed that his intelligence was unusual, others that his power was supernatural; so that some had limitless veneration for him, others an unaccountable dread. Students all over the country looked on him as an uncrowned king (8).

But what is detestable in him is that he persists in exposing the lives of innocent young men and women to danger to gain personal ends even when he very well knows that his "enterprise" is doomed to failure. Supporting his own role he declares:

> I've long given up thinking in terms of victory and defeat. As leader in a grand enterprise I'm here because it becomes me; either victory or defeat will be equally great..... On a historical view, the epic may seem to end in a vast burial ground of defeat. Still it would be an epic. For the curtailed manhood of this slave-ridden country, isn't it the greatest of opportunities to be able to die the death of a hero? (21-22).

About his conduct and mentality Rajendra Verma records:

> Here is the psychology of a frustrated man who is out to avenge it on society. His megalomania, like that of the modern dictators, is the result of inner and outer maladjustment in the personal life which seeks a certain rationalization in abnormal or dramatic conduct.[57]

Tagore depicts the ramifications of the revolutionary organisation of Indranath with convincing accuracy to the situation in Bengal in the opening years of this century.

Indranath's relations with his followers overstep the claims of politics and in fact intrude into their emotional and personal lives. In the novel, he is often referred to as the "Master" who holds complete sway over his followers and demands implicit obedience from them. Describing the terrorist leaders, known in Bengal as "dadas," Gordon writes:

> In addition to his primary function as a political leader, the dada seems to hold something of the neoparental authority which the older brother would exercise in a Bengali family.... The relationship also seems to reflect an important religious concept: the guru-shishya relationship where the disciple is to give his complete loyalty, devotion, and respect to his teacher.[58]

Now, Ela-Atin love affair comes under the disapproving gaze of the Master, who at the time of initiating Ela into the movement had cautioned her against any emotional entanglements. He gave her this instruction:

> The only promise I ask of you is never to become entangled in any social relationship. You are not for society, but for your country alone! (12).

His close surveillance of them reveals that both are disenchanted with the movement and also that nothing but death would keep them apart. He also knows that they are about to be betrayed by Batu, one of the terrorists who is jealous of Atin. Indranath exhibits his evil genius in directing Atin to liquidate Ela before she falls into the hands of the police. There is no indication in the novel, concerned as it is solely with the love of Ela and Atin, about the final outcome of the movement directed by Indranath but what Tagore seems to suggest is that out of a creed which is infected at the source itself nothing good can come at all.

In the beginning of the novel Ela has been drawn into the movement by her idealism and love for the country. She is put in charge of a high school for girls established by Indranath but her main function is to act as a magnet to attract impressionable young men into the movement. Responding to her complain for not giving her any revolutionary work, the Master replies:

> It's not work I want of you. Of course, it is hardly possible for you yourself to know of the glory that lights up the hearts of the boys at the touch of your fingers when you anoint their foreheads with the red sandal-paste of initiation. How can the dry rewards I have to offer evoke the same quality of work? Where sex works I put woman on a pedestal (13).

The truth of the Master's words is revealed by the entry of Atin, a gifted young man, into the party. He takes its vows not for its sake but for Ela. He is not like the other hare-brained youth in the terrorist fold and is able to see through its facade the reality of patriotic work. He tells Ela:

> The new birth, the new age, the gate of death—all these tags sicken me so! The members of the band have tried their best to paint me with their brush, but I've not been able to take their colour (72).

Though Ela feels attracted to Atin the moment she sets eyes on him but her pledge to the Master prevents her from reciprocating his love. She confesses to Atin:

> I had already sworn to devote myself to my country, not to keep anything for myself alone. My betrothal was to my country (30-31).

But protesting her remark Atin says:

> The pledge of yours was a crime and, every day you keep it, you commit a fresh outrage against your own nature. To crush under the heels of your party a feeling which is of the purest, which comes by command of the Creator Himself, is a sin for which you'll have to take punishment (31).

Atin's such revelations of the nature of terrorist activities have shaken Ela's implicit faith in Indranath, and so she feels free to reciprocate his love in the following words:

> I offer you my hand in marriage, Ontu, as the princesses of old used to do. Take me. There's no time to lose. Let us pledge our troth by exchange of vows. Then take me as helpmate along your path (64).

However, Ela-Atin romantic envolvement cannot escape from the attention of Indranath, who is inclined to tolerate it as they do not wish to crown it with marriage. In his usual flamboyant manner he declares:

> ....I've no use either for ascetics who mortify their bodies with sackcloth and ashes or for self-immolators who reduce to ashes their natural passions. We want fire-worshippers, but if any of these kindle the fire within themselves, they have to be got rid of. Our conflagration must rage throughout the land, and that cannot be achieved with those whose fire has gone out, or those who cannot control their own flame (II).

Indranath, with this pronouncement, turns down Ela's plea to be relieved from her obligations. As regards Atin, Indranath is certain that his sense of honour and self-respect will keep him on till the end, despite his doubts about the movement.

But Indranath's calculations prove wrong. He under-estimates the degree of disillusionment in the two lovers as regards the "meanness, unfaithfulness, mutual mistrust, secret machination, plotting for leadership" (63) which made a place for themselves among the revolutionaries. Atin particularly questions the very philosophy of terrorism. He explains to Ela the situation before them:

> One who openly fights a more powerful foe, even if his be a hopeless struggle, is in the same class as his opponent; his honour remains unsullied..... It was for us before we were knocked out, before we met our death, to prove ourselves the greater, as men—why—else this play of pitting ourselves against immeasurably superior forces? ....One thing had become clear to me. To oppose

> overwhelming strength by brute force can but brutalise in the end one's very soul (61-62).

Sharing Atin's disillusionment Ela confesses:

> I must confess, Ontu, that lately the terrible tragedy of it has been revealed to me also. I had entered the lists at the call of glory, but the shame of it is enveloping me more and more. Tell me, what we can do now? (62-63).

To it Atin replies:

> Every man and woman is called upon to fight the great fight in the field of righteousness, where to die is to earn the highest heaven. But, for us, the way to that battlefield is closed. We must now reap to the end the fruits of our past Karma, our past deeds (63).

Both Atin and Ela are too deeply enmeshed in the movement to escape and Atin does not wish to desert his comrades who are as much in peril as he. So Atin significantly remarks:

> There's no way out now. The arrow can miss the mark but it cannot return to the quiver (64).

Disillusionment and the moment of awareness come to Atin very early, but he retains his loyalty to the cause. Indranath informs Ela of Atin's loyalty. To quote Indranath:

> He remains bound by his own resolve. I know he'll never be rid of his doubts. At every step his finer feelings will be hurt. And yet his self-respect will keep him on till the end (16).

Atin acknowledges and obeys Indranath's commands implicitly even when he is ordered to cut off his relations with Ela, for whose sake he had thrown himself into the vortex of terrorism. When Ela unexpectedly turns up at his secret hideout and remonstrates against his obedience to the Master's mandate not to meet her, justifying himself Atin says:

> Tremendous longing crushed me in its coils day and night, but I won't give in. They had put me down as sentimental; they were so certain that in the day of trial

> I'd be found to be made of clay ! It was beyond them to understand that in my sentiments lay my strength (52).

The frequent meetings between Ela and Atin afford them an opportunity to renew their oaths of love but provoke Indranath's ire. Earlier when Atin visits Ela's house, a message is sent to him through a note written on red paper to immediately quit the house without a word to her and he at once does so because he could not disregard the command of the Master. Again, when Ela comes to his hideout, he is warned of danger and rushes out, ignoring her pleas not to leave her behind. After Atin leaves, Indranath unexpectedly arrives and orders her to go back at once to her rooms, threatening that had it been wise to kill her, he would have done so then and there itself. These two incidents make him feel that their love has become a threat to the movement and he resolves to liquidate Ela and entrusts the task to Atin himself who is all for her.

Taking this message Atin goes to Ela's place. The message is:

> The word has gone forth from your own band—your beloved, patriotic brothers, whom you've anointed with sandalpaste on each Brother's Day—that you're not fit to live any longer (84).

Then Atin informs Ela how he had been brought down to the last rung of degradation by being made an accessory in the murder of an old helpless widow for her money and how Batu had ensured that he would be arrested any moment. Ela kisses him and entreats him thus:

> Kill me, Ontu, kill me with your own hands. I couldn't wish for a happier end.... Don't have any qualms. Am I not yours, wholly yours, even in death ? Take me. Don't let their unclean hands touch my body, for this body belongs to you (85-86).

The novel ends on a moving note along with a thin sound of whistle indicating that the police have raided the hideout of the terrorists:

> Atin took hold of her arm and drew her down with him to her bedroom. "Get into bed at once," he repeated, "and go off to sleep."
>
> "I can't, sleep won't come."
>
> "I've brought medicine that'll put you to sleep."
>
> "What's the use of that, Ontu? Let the last bit of my consciousness be for you. Is it chloroform that you leave? Throw it away. I'm not a coward. Let me die awake, in your arms. Let our last kiss be eternal, Ontu, my Ontu."
>
> From afar came the thin sound of whistle (86).

K.R. Srinivasa Iyengar aptly compares Atin and Ela to Yuri and Lara in Doctor Zhivago and comments:

> They are a trapped pair, these doomed lovers; but they do not wince. Nothing in their lives, became them so well as their end.[59]

Bimanbehari Mazumdar rightly comments:

> Ela is the bravest of all the heroines drawn by Rabindranath..... No other heroine of Rabindranath is so outspoken and analytical as Ela.[60]

Through the sacrifice of Atin and Ela at the altar of the Juggernaut of terrorism, Tagore vindicates the superior principle of human love which conquers the meanness, cruelty, and horror of a blind and inhuman machine which seeks to crush whatever is fine and noble in human life. The novelist's critique of misconceived and misdirected revolutionary activity is clearly reflected in what he records about Atin:

> Where was the truth, the valour, the glory in it? From the mire of masked robberies and murder into which the movement had progressively been drawn, no pillar of light would ever rise to illumine the pages of history. With his god-given gifts destroyed, Atin could now see no prospect of fruition before him, but rather the certain vanquishment of his self. Defeat has its value, but not the

> defeat of soul that brings in its train ghastly doings underground, unmeaning unending... (50-51).

As the title suggests, the novel comprises of four chapters, each chapter devoted to a particular phase of Atin-Ela relationship. The first chapter opening in a tea-shop, a rendezvous of revolutionaries, depicts the apprehensions of Ela about Atin and traces the background of Indranath, using the flashback technique. In the second chapter locating in Ela's rooms, the novelist interrupts the course of action to interpolate an account of the first meeting of Atin and Ela four years earlier. In the third chapter placed in a secret hide-out of Atin, we are provided with the points of view of Atin and Ela about their terrorist activities and their growing disenchantment with them. In the final chapter taking place in Ela's rooms, there is again the use of flashback to recollect the initiation of Atin into the movement three years earlier through a symbolic birthday party. Extensive use of dialogue to reveal character and device of flashback to depict dove-tailing of present and past incidents makes the novel a popular one.

Humayun Kabir feels that the novel, in spite of its lyric quality and brilliance of language, "leaves us with a sense of incompleteness and dissatisfaction."[61]

To sum up, *Four Chapters*, in spite of various protesting comments from different critics, can be viewed in the nationalist perspective since the three main characters are developed along with the growth of terrorist movement for the country's freedom that runs parallel to the growth of Atin-Ela romantic love which ultimately defeat death in the form of sacrifice.

REFERENCES

1. Mehta, P.P., *Indo-Anglian Fiction: An Assessment* (Bareilly: Prakash Book Depot, 1979), 28.
2. Ghose, Sisirkumar, *Rabindranath Tagore* (New Delhi: Sahitya Akademi, 1994), 72.
3. Raj, G.V. *Tagore: The Novelist* (New Delhi: Sterling Publishers Pvt. Ltd., 1983), 40.

4. Kabir, Humayun, *The Bengali Novel* (Calcutta: Firma K.L. Mukhopadhyay, 1968), 41.
5. Ray, Niharranjan, "Three Novels of Tagore," *Indian Literature*, IV (New Delhi: Sahitya Akademi, 1961), 170.
6. Sen, Sukumar, "*History of Bengali Literature*, (New Delhi: Sahitya Akademi, 1960), 313.
7. Ray, Annada Sankar, "Tolstoy and Tagore," *Indian Literature*, IV, (1961), 77.
8. Kripalani, Krishna, *Tagore: A Life*, rev. ed. (New Delhi: Orient Longmans Ltd., 1971), 118.
9. Kripalani, Krishna, *Rabindranath Tagore: A Biography* (London: Oxford University Press, 1962), 207.
10. Bhattacharya, Bhabani, "Tagore as Novelist" in *Rabindranath Tagore: A Centenary Volume*, 1861-1961 (New Delhi: Sahitya Akademi, 1961), 97.
11. Ray, Niharranjan, "Three Novels of Tagore," *Indian Literature*, IV, 172.
12. Kripalani, Krishna, *Rabindranath Tagore: A Biography*, 208.
13. Kabir, Humayun, *The Bengali Novel*, 45.
14. Ray, Niharranjan, "Three Novels of Tagore," *Indian Literature*, IV, 172.
15. Mukherjee, Sujit, *Passage to America* (Calcutta: Bookland Private Ltd., 1964), 181.
16. Kripalani, Krishna, *Tagore: A Life*, 118.
17. *Gora*, transl. W.W. Pearson from *Gora* (1910). London: Macmillan, 1924; rpt. Madras: Macmillan, 1976, 22. All subsequent references in parentheses are to this rpt. Madras, 1976.
18. Bhattacharya, Bhabani, "Tagore as a Novelist" in *Rabindranath Tagore: 1861-1961: A Centenary Volume* (New Delhi: Sahitya Akademi, 1961), 98.
19. Chakravorty, B.C., *Rabindranath Tagore: His Mind and Art* (New Delhi: Young India Publications, 1971), 108.
20. Chaudhuri, Nirad C., "Tagore and the Nobel Prize," *Illustrated Weekly of India*," March 1973, 15.
21. Mukherjee, S., *Passage to America*, 181.
22. Sen Gupta, S.C., *The Great Sentinel: A Study of Rabindranath Tagore* (Calcutta: A Mukherjee, 1948), 219.
23. Raj, G.V., *Tagore: The Novelist* (New Delhi: Sterling Publishers Pvt. Ltd., 1983), 47.

24. *Ibid.*, 50.
25. Ray, Niharranjan, *Three Novels of Tagore*, 170.
26. Tagore, Rabindranath, "A Hymn to India," *Indian Literatures*, Vol. 1, No. 2 (Apr.-Sept., 1958), 3.
27. Iyengar, Srinivasa, K.R., *Rabindranath Tagore* (New Delhi: Sterling Publishers Pvt. Ltd., 1987), 88.
28. Raizada, Harish, "Humanism in the Novels of Rabindranath Tagore" in *Perspectives on Rabindranath Tagore*, ed. T.R. Sharma (Ghaziabad: Vimal Prakashan, 1986), 70.
29. Majumdar, Bimanbehari, *Heroines of Tagore* (Calcutta: Firma, K.L. Mukhopadhyay, 1968), 246.
30. Kripalani, Krishna, *Rabindranath Tagore* (London: Oxford University Press, 1962), 252.
31. Srinivasa Iyengar, K.R., *Rabindranath Tagore* (Bombay: Popular Prakashan, 1965), 84.
32. Forster, E.M., "Two Books by Tagore" in *Abinger Harvest* (1936): rpt. Pocket Edition (London: Edwin Arnold and Co., 1953), 366.
33. Cited in Rathindranath Tagore, *On the Edges of Time* (New Delhi: Orient Longmans, 1958), 72.
34. Sarkar, Samit, *The Swadeshi Movement in Bengal* (New Delhi: People's Publishing House, 1973), 91.
35. Ray, Niharranjan, *An Artist in Life: A Commentary on the Life and Works of Rabindranath Tagore* (Trivandrum: University of Kerala, 1967), 233.
36. Bhattacharya, Bhabani, "Tagore as a Novelist," in *Rabindranath Tagore 1861-1961. A Centenary Volume* (New Delhi: Sahitya Akademi, 1961), 99.
37. Kripalani, Krishna, *Rabindranath Tagore*, 178.
38. *The Home and the World*, Transl. Surendranath Tagore from *Ghare-Baire* (1916). (London: Macmillan, 1919; rpt. Madras: Macmillan, 1976), 122. All subsequent references in parentheses are to this edition.
39. Naravane, V.S., *An Introduction to Rabindranath Tagore* (Delhi: Macmillan, 1977), 119.
40. Khanolkar, G.D., *The Lute and the Plough*, Trans. thomas Gay (Bombay: The Book Centre Pvt. Ltd., 1963), 190.
41. Thomson, Edward, *Rabindranath Tagore, Poet and Dramatist* (London: O.U.P., 1948), 246.

42. Bhaskar, R.P., "The Novels of Tagore" in *The Genius of Tagore: Tagore Centenanry Volume, Part I*, ed. Mahendra Kulasreshta (Hoshiarpur: V.V.R. Institute, 1961), 100.
43. Chakravorty, B.C., *Rabindranath Tagore: His Mind and Art* (New Delhi: Young India Publications, 1971), 207.
44. Raj, G.V., *Tagore: The Novelist* (New Delhi: Sterling Publishers P. Ltd., 1983), 62.
45. *Ibid.*, 63.
46. Kripalani, Krishna, *Rabindranath Tagore*, 252.
47. Sen, Sukumar, *History of Bengali Literature* (1960; rpt. New Delhi: Sahitya Akademi, 1979), 285.
48. Tagore, Rabindranath, *Four Chapters*, Transl. Surendranath Tagore. (1950, rpt. Calcutta: Visva-Bharati,1961). Author's note transl. Somnath Maitra and Kanti Chandrasen, P.V. All subsequent references in parentheses are to this edition.
49. Ghose, Sisirkumar, *Rabindranath Tagore* (New Delhi: Sahitya Akademi, 1994), 79.
50. Kabir, Humayun, *The Bengali Novel* (Calcutta: Firma K.L. Mukhopadhyay, 1968), 55.
51. Iyengar, K.R.S., *Rabindranath Tagore* (New Delhi: Sterling Publishers Pvt. Ltd., 1987), 93-94.
52. Sen, Sukumar, *History of Bengali Literature* (New Delhi: Sahitya Akademi, 1979), 286.
53. Gordon, Leonard A., *Bengal: The Nationalist Movement* 1876-1940 (Delhi: Manohar Book Service, 1974), 157-58.
54. Sinha, Sasadhar, *Social Thinking of Rabindranath Tagore* (Bombay: Asia Publishing House, 1962), 114-15.
55. *Ibid.*, 117-18. Translation of the Preface by Sasadhar Sinha.
56. Bannerjee, Srikumar, "Rabindranath's Novels" in *Homage to Rabindranath Tagore*, ed. B.M. Chaudhuri (Kharagpur: Indian Institute of Technology, 1961), 85.
57. Verma, Rajendra, *Rabindranath Tagore: Prophet Against Totalitarianism* (Bombay: Asia Publishing House, 1964), 18.
58. *Ibid.*, 142.
59. Iyengar, Srinivasa K.R., *Indian Writing in English* (New Delhi: Sterling Publishers Pvt. Ltd., 1984), 109.
60. Mazumdar, Bimanbehari, *Heroines of Tagore* (Calcutta: Firma K.L. Mukhopadhyay, 1968), 282.
61. Kabir, Humayun, *The Bengali Novel*, 56.

5

Conclusion

TAGORE'S FINAL VISION OF LIFE AND MAN

Rabindranath Tagore, a many-faceted and many splendoured genius—as poet, philosopher, prophet, patriot, painter, musician, mystic, novelist, essayist and educationist, rests his final vision of life and man on liberal humanism and universality. Whatever else Tagore might have been, he was above everything else a great humanist and universalist—a true citizen of the world. He believed in one world and in the eternal vision of man evolving into an All-man, Vishva-Manava. He felt that the West and the East had much to teach each other. "Human values were essentially the same in the West and the East. Human values were more to him than power values, the 'spirit of man' more than the power and the glory of the nation."[1]

Rabindranath looks at man both from within and from outside. As a greater species of creation, he thinks that the great power within man ignites him to play his role for emancipation of himself through emancipation of the whole of mankind. He introspects that the way of freedom for man is that of the feeling of the divine presence of God who makes him. To him, the true concept of the nature of man is in realisation of steadfastness to truth and cultivation of courtesy, simplicity and other virtues that mirror the true culture of man as a social being. The dehumanisation of man as seen in all ugliness in all affairs of life has pained Tagore. The best of man as Tagore rightly thinks suffers terribly because the best of his thoughts die unborn and unexpressed. For a man to be a "man," his role of taking part in eternity by means of his uniqueness is infinite. Tagore wants to give freedom to have a significant role in the concept of man.

Tagore thinks that the real "man" lost in the melee of mechanisation, automation and artificialities indicates a massacre of human sensibilities. The release of the obsessions within and unison with the infinite is what Tagore highlights as the essential concept of man. It is a submission of man to the altar of the Eternity, the Ever Present that makes man worthy of himself.

To be one with the world with all its diversities is what Tagore defines as the ideal concept of man. While defining the endless power of the Eternal spirit that remains in unison with man, Tagore makes a revolutionary approach to the oneness of things that highlights the glory of man. Tagore profoundly believes in upholding man as the true image of God. The concept of man so related to God brings forth another Tagorean dimension of the uniqueness of man. It is oneness of man and God. As Radhakrishnan explains:

> With the annihilation of the ego comes the fulfilment of love. The self-centred life becomes God-centred. Man shall not see god and live, goes the saying. Certainly not. So long as he is man he cannot see Him. When he sees Him he ceases to be man.[2]

In all his novels studied in the above chapters, Tagore emphasises the importance of man above all types of orthodoxy, narrow-minded sectarianism, religion, parochialism and violence. Dr. Harish Raizada comments:

> ...he asserts his unswerving faith in the joy of life, freedom of the individual, respect for human personality, man's obedience to his conscience and his enjoyment of life through love and sacrifice—the universal virtues which stands for humanism in life.[3]

In fact, Tagore treated the problems of his age from the intellectual and philosophical point of view and hence more profoundly. He could see real man stripped of all prejudices and biases and as an incarnation of divinity on earth. It is this assertion of the importance of man and human values above everything else that gives Tagore and his novels a unique place in Indian literature.

As a living legend in his own time, Tagore projected an image of his personality in which the myth and the man seemed inseparable. A keen aliveness to the happenings around him was one of his strong points and he exhibited to the end of his life a deep interest in all matters concerning his country and the world at large.

Tagore's philosophy of life is based on his emphasis on the development of the human personality and in his deep set conviction there is no inherent contradiction between the claims of the so-called opposites — the flesh and the spirit, the human and the divine, love of life and love of God, joy in beauty and pursuit of truth, social obligation and individual rights, respect for tradition and the freedom to experiment, love of onc's people and faith in the unity of mankind. These seeming opposites can and must be reconciled, not by tentative compromises and timid vacillation but by building a true harmony out of the apparent discordance.

He loved this earth too well to turn away from it. He was human and humane, a fully developed man responding to both the joy of life and the cry of human distress. He was a lover of his people and his loyalty was pledged to all mankind. All his life he stood and strove for social justice, equality, material well-being of the poor, self-government of the citizens, education for the ignorant mass, unfettered development of children and equal status of woman with man. He was a preacher of the religion of man; his renunciation was of the base passions of cupidity and hatred and he fought for the freedom of the human personality from all that strangles it.

Tagore was a pioneer in the field of education. He emphasised on what we all know today that what the child imbibes at home and in school is far more important than what he studies at college. He also emphasised on teaching through mother-tongue, practical classes, training of all the senses and preference of culture to academic knowledge. Even Mahatma Gandhi adopted Tagore's scheme of Community Development after many years. Indeed, he was a great nation-builder. He believed in the power and resources of science but he dreaded every form of organised power, whether social, political or industrial, which ignored human values and tended to stifle the personality of man. He opines that man needs both machine and organisation for his welfare, but they must be mastered and humanised by him instead of his being mechanised and dehumanised by them. Krishna Kripalani says that the world should be grateful to Tagore whose genius was so consistently dedicated to the good of humanity.

Regarding Tagore's idea of nationalism it can be said that he emphasised on the formation of one world and one nation of the mankind. In this sense he was an internationalist. He had a clear and steady vision of man's destiny and an unerring instinct for those first principles which if men and nations betray, they perish at the root. To him the need to understand values other than those which have come to be identified with one's own way of living is the greatest moral challenge with which the world is faced today.

Tagore delineates his heroines and woman characters as displaying a rare assurance and psychological strength. Through a variety of perspectives, he depicts their search for identity or realisation of self-fulfilment within the bounds of tradition and society. Commenting on Tagore's outlook on woman in Indian society, Edward Thompson writes:

> He would have her remain woman—a centre of love and inspiration without which the world is poverty-stricken. But he has never ceased to attack the justice and cruelty which regard woman as inferior or unfitted for education of the arts.[4]

Thus, while conveying the feelings of tenderness and devotion, traditionally associated with Indian womanhood, he depicts their struggle against discrimination and ill-usage, as can be seen from *Binodini, Gora* and *Chaturanga*. Except in *Gora* the dominant character in each novel happens to be a woman who is projected as an index of the Indian psyche, responding to the new social ontology and emerging from her shell to take her rightful place in society. She does not always succeed but her very efforts betoken her innate nobility and spirit of sacrificial heroism.

Tagores novels as a whole suggest an emerging pattern seeking to encompass his vision of Indian reality and his adumbration of ideas about the nature of Indian society and culture caught up in the throes of radical change. Tagore's distinctiveness lies in his responding positively to the forces of historical acceleration in Indian milieu without abandoning the age-old values which are inseparable from the Indian social life. His novels carry the investigation further by being set in the present, in order that a deepening perspective is realised as the issues acquire contemporary relevance. The interest that informs his novels is chiefly anchored in the struggle of his principal characters, particularly his women characters, to achieve self-actualisation or self-definition. Tagore's novelistic world embodies a vision of India caught up in the cross-currents of opposing ideologies, of the questioning of the old or traditional moral sanctions in search of self-fulfilment, the clash between the reformist and revivalist forces, the conflict between the moderate and the extremist elements in politics as well as the eternal struggle in the human consciousness between love and sacrifice.

It is evident from these novels which span nearly four decades of Tagore's literary career that he has been extraordinarily successful in projecting a realistic image of Indian society in transition or in the throes of a struggle to cope with a troubled social order. It is not usually realised that it is as a novelist that Tagore grappled with issues that have influenced the very character of the Indian society.

TAGORE'S POSITION AMONG THE INDIAN WRITERS

Tagore was the central figure in the creative awakening that synchronised with what is termed as the Indian Renaissance—an awakening that witnessed the genesis of the novel in India. Not only did the Renaissance affect a remarkable change in the attitude of the Indian intelligentsia towards the problem of human existence by precipitating new critical attitude, but it also ushered in an efflorescence of literatures in Indian languages by the transplantation of new literary genres from Europe. Rabindranath Tagore may be said to exemplify its climax with his extraordinary nexus of talents and gifts—as poet, playwright, philosopher, painter, composer, novelist, short story writer, educationist, culture hero, and a reconciler of indigenous and foreign traditions.

Rabindranath Tagore is taken as the father of Indian novels. While Krishna Kripalani and T.W. Clark opine that Bankim Chandra Chatterjee was the first Indian novelist, Mulk Raj Anand strongly differs from this view and has designated Rabindranath Tagore as "the first novelist of India."[5] In fact, it is as a celebrant and threnodist of the glory of pre-Moghul and pre-British Bengal that the chief excellence of Bankim Chandra Chatterjee lies and not as the creator of the modern novel, the credit for which must go to Rabindranath Tagore. Commenting on the indiscriminate adulation, set in motion by the award of the Nobel Prize to Tagore, E.M. Forster observed in a review of CHITRA in 1914: "He is a good writer. All must assent to this minimum. But how good? To this, there can be no answer until the adoration, and the reaction all adoration entails, have passed away."[6] More recently, Sisirkumar Ghose has rightly pointed out that "Superficial adulation, or, as recently, superficial criticism has blunted the edge of keen sensibility and we have to be content with partial or even partisan reviews."[7]

TAGORE'S POPULARITY, INTERNATIONAL FAME AND RECOGNITION

Rabindranath Tagore's popularity lies in his use of many innovative techniques of novel writing. He was the first Indian novelist to use the flashback technique in the structuring of narrative. He was the first novelist to employ multiple points of view (as in *The Home and the World*) and "central consciousness" (as in *Chaturanga*). This invests them with a kind of psychological realism which Bankim's novels lack. He was the first in using narration in the first person. This helped him in eliminating authorial intervention. Another instance of his innovative bias can be seen in his heavy reliance on dialogue to intensify the dramatic effect of his novels. Indeed, several scenes from his novels seem fit for stage representation, needing no adaptation whatsoever.

Tagore remains a pioneer in initiating the psychological novel based on social reality and in bringing out the nuances of change in his major characters through their interaction with circumstances. His novels mark the transition from the tradition of historical romance which characterised the Indian novel upto his time to the realistic tradition that has set in with him. It is Tagore who ushered in the spirit of social realism and liberal humanism into the Indian novel and it is to him that the modern Indo-Anglian novel owes its moral and humane concern in its projection of contemporary reality. His themes are formed out of the matrix of social and emotional life. The predicament of the Indian woman, the clash between the orthodox and the progressive, the right consciousness of national heritage, and the conflict of values in a changing life style are important themes of Tagore's novels.

As a many-splendoured genius, a national and international celebrity and the Grand old Man of Indian letters, Rabindranath Tagore's writings merit our serious study and no assessment of his literary achievement can be complete without an appraisal of his novels which "offer an intellectual and aesthetic middle ground, as it were, holding in exquisite balance the sensitive truths of the private vision and the solid varieties of the public experience."[8] As one who naturalised the new literary genre of the novel by blazing new trails in theme and technique, Rabindranath Tagore deserves to be recognised as the real initiator of the modern novel in India.

Tagore came as a harmoniser and he strove to build a durable bridge of understanding between man and nature, man and machine, man and God. He not only spanned the ages of Indian history with his melodies, he also tried to annul the yawning divide of culture and civilisation, the antinomy between what Sir Charles Snow has called the "two cultures"—humanistic wisdom and scientific knowledge. He was a Titanic force in life and literature, and his example gave Indians and Asians both self-respect and self-confidence, and showed them the way to self-mastery and self-realisation. Giving a tribute to Rabindranath Tagore Dr. K.R.S. Iyengar writes:

> He tirelessly pursued the ideal of Beauty, and Beauty was to him also Love, Truth, Goodness and Power. In poem or play or story or novel, in reminiscence or exegesis or exhortation or prophecy, Tagore is essentially of a piece, and the total impact of his life and work is indeed that of a modern Leonardo da Vinci, of a multiple power and personality.[9]

After the Tagore Centenary Celebrations are over, some good work of permanent significance has doubtless come out of the centenary celebrations, and we are duly grateful, not only for the bibliographies, translations and biographical studies, but also for the production of some of the plays, and for the symposia and the seminars. Apart from the government-sponsored celebrations, there has also been witnessed a spontaneous burst of salutation on an almost global scale from individual lovers of freedom, poetry and culture, and this really is the measure of the large space Tagore fills in the treasured memories of the human race. Offerings have come from the "four ends of the world"—from Denmark, from Mauritius, from Trinidad, from the Philippines.

Of the commemorative tomes, the most sumptuous, perhaps, is the one brought out by the Sahitya Akademi: *Rabindranath Tagore: A Centenary Volume*, 1861-1961. It includes a "chronicle" by Kshitis Roy and a "bibliography" by Jagadindra Baumik, and there are also illustrations and facsimiles of Tagore manuscripts. The list of contributors and the table of contents give a sense of global participation in the undertaking. Not only Tagore's son, Rathindranath, and his niece, Indira Devi Chaudhurani, but many others as well who had known the poet or worked with him join in pooling their "memories" together to enable the perceptive reader to form a picture of the "whole" man. Recalling her predicament during the nineteen twenties, Madame Ocampo, who knew Tagore and had seen Gandhiji remarks:

> The Mahatma on one side, the poet on the other. Many of us did not know whom to prefer, whom to admire more.

Pearl Buck salutes Tagore as a "world poet" whose words were charged with beauty "comprehending not only love of God and relationship between man and God but human love." Prof. Tucci of Rome recalls how his contacts with Tagore gave him "an idea of what the Rishis of old could have been." Ben Van Eysselstein mentions an anecdote of the poet disarming a child's fears with a smile:

> "Words were for them superfluous. A smile sufficed. And is not a tranquil smile the beginning and end of all wisdom?"

When Tagore was in Urbana in 1912-13, he seems to have made such a deep impression on his friends that one of them, Mrs. Bessie Smith, has remarked: "He had the most beautiful eyes I've ever seen. The whole world seemed to be in his eyes." And a Frankfurt newspaper recorded forty years ago: "Tagore is a longing personified."

Tagore is compared with Goethe and Leonardo by many scholars. Toshihito Katayama of Japan remarks:

> The intuition of the living Unity joins with the vision of the eternal human in the thoughts of Tagore and Goethe. The realisation of potential life may naturally and by necessity bring into flower a pure humanity.[10]

Sunilchandra Sarkar is of the opinion that in his "power of acute and manifold reception" Tagore recalls men like Goethe and Leonardo. Alexandra Philippide, the Roumanian poet, compares Tagore with Goethe and other great literary figures whose work "while bearing the stamp of a national character, also had the features of universality, including human features that are essential in all ages and places." Taraknath Sen, again, remarks that Goethe and Tagore "belong to the same order of mind and community of spirit.... In both, a noble physical presence combined with a mind of unique breadth and depth and of a far-reaching vision gave them a prophet's command over their age; prophet-like, too, both have garnered and handed down values that posterity would not willingly let die." D.S. Sarma hails Tagore as the "Leonardo da Vinci of the Indian Renaissance" and Anders Osterling finds in both Tagore and Goethe "the objectivity of the productive man, the non-party man's demand to be allowed to rise in his defence." Tagore is crowned as the "Goethe of India" by Albert Schweitzer. Krishna Kripalani remarks that Tagore's contribution to the Indian history is subtler and deeper than that of Gandhi, for it released and fed the hidden fountains of creative activity in fields which the politician is powerless to exploit.

Giving a tribute to Tagore Mahatma Gandhi called him the Great sentinel, the conscience of his people whose voice never failed to protest against any injustice or wrong; and the greatest poet of the age. Gandhi wrote: "There was hardly any public activity on which he has not left the impress of his powerful personality." "He was the greatest figure of the modern Indian Renaissance."[11] In fact, he was in the grand line from Valmiki and Kalidasa. Sarojini Naidu, the Indian poetess, wrote: "By his genius, his beauty, his wisdom and wit, the charm and prestige of his gracious personality, he was in his lifetime a unique and fascinating figure of romance. Now that he has gone he will become an exquisite legend, a fairy tale for all time."[12] With him, it seemed, died an age. In his tribute to Tagore, Jawaharlal Nehru says that Tagore was not narrowly national. His message was for the world. Yet he was one hundred per cent India's child, and the inheritor, representative and expositor of her age-long culture.

REFERENCES

1. Iyengar, K.R. Srinivasa, *Rabindranath Tagore: A Critical Introduction* (New Delhi: Sterling Publishers Pvt. Ltd., 1987), 106-107.
2. Radhakrishnan, S., *The Philosophy of Rabindranath Tagore* (Baroda: Good Companions Publishers, 1961), 38.
3. Raizada, Harish, "Humanism in the Novels of Rabindranath Tagore" in T.R. Sharma ed. *Perspectives on Rabindranath Tagore* (Ghaziabad: Vimal Prakashan, 1986), 78.
4. Thompson, Edward, *Rabindranath Tagore: His Life and Works*, rev. by Kalidas Nag (Calcutta: Y.M.C.A. Publishing House, 1961), 74-75.
5. Anand, Mulk Raj, "Tagore and Indian Renaissance" in *The Genius of Tagore: Tagore Centenary Volume, Part I*, ed. Mahendra Kulasreshta. (Hoshiarpur: V.V.R. Institute, 1961), 67.
6. Forster, E.M., *Abinger Harvest* (London: Edwin Arnold, 1936), 363.
7. Ghose, Sisirkumar, *The Later Poems of Tagore* (Bombay: Asia Publishing House, 1961), 13.
8. Krishna Rao, A.V., *The Indo-Anglian Novel and the Changing Tradition* (Mysore: Rao and Raghavan, 1972), 12.
9. Iyengar, K.R.S., *Rabindranath Tagore: A Critical Introduction*, 112.
10. *Ibid.*, 2.
11. Kripalani, Krishna, *Rabindranath Tagore: A Biography* (Calcutta: Visva-Bharati, Revd. ed., 1980), 453.
12. *Ibid.*, 455.

Select Bibliography

PRIMARY SOURCES

Novels

Binodini. Transl. Krishna Kripalani from *Chokher Bali* (1903), New Delhi: Sahitya Akademi, 1959.

The Wreck. Transl. J.G. Drummond from *Nauka Dubi* (1906). London: Macmillan, 1921; rpt. Madras: Macmillan, 1975.

Gora. Transl. W.W. Pearson from *Gora* (1910). London: Macmillan, 1924; rpt. Madras: Macmillan, 1976.

The Home and the World. Transl. Surendranath Tagore from *Ghare-Baire* (1916). London: Macmillan, 1919; rpt. Madras: Macmillan, 1976.

Chaturanga. Transl. Ashok Mitra from *Chaturanga* (1916). New Delhi: Sahitya Akademi, 1963.

Farewell, My Friend. Transl. Krishna Kripalani from *Sesher Kavita* (1929). London: The New India Publishing Company, 1949; Bombay: Jaico Publishing House, 1956; rpt. 1966.

Two Sisters. Transl. Krishna Kripalani from *Dui Bon* (1933), Calcutta: Visva-Bharati, 1945; rpt. 1964.

The Garden. Transl. Krishna Kripalani from *Malancha* (1934). Included in *Farewell, My Friend and the Garden.* Bombay: Jaico Publishing House, 1956; rpt. 1966.

Four Chapters. Transl. Surendranath Tagore from *Char Adhayay* (1934). Calcutta: Visva-Bharati, 1950; rpt. 1961.

Other Works

Collected Poems and Plays of Rabindranath Tagore. London: Macmillan & Co., 1936; rpt. 1955.

Creative Unity. London: Macmillan and Co., 1922; rpt. 1959.

Glimpses of Bengal. Madras: Macmillan, 1921; rpt. 1960.

Lectures and Addresses. Ed. Anthony X. Soares. Madras: Macmillan, 1950.

Letters to Friend. London: Allen and Unwin, 1928.

My Reminiscences. Madras: Macmillan, 1917; rpt. 1960.

Nationalism. Madras: Macmillan, 1917; rpt. 1976.

On Art and Aesthetics. Ed. Prithwish Neogy. Calcutta: Orient Longmans, 1961.

Personality. Madras: Macmillan, 1917; rpt. 1959.

Sadhana. Madras: Macmillan, 1913; rpt. 1979.

The Religion of Man. London: Allen and Unwin, 1931.

Towards Universal Man. Bombay: Asia Publishing House, 1961.

SECONDARY SOURCES

Anand, Mulk Raj. *Homage to Tagore.* Lahore: Sangam Publication Ltd., 1946.

——. "Modern Indian Fiction." In *Indian Annual Review,* 1954. New Delhi: Information Service of India, 1954.

——. "Tagore and Indian Renaissance." In *The Genius of Tagore: Tagore Centenary Volume, Part I,* ed. Mahendra Kulasreshta, Hoshiarpur: V.V.R. Institute, 1961.

——. "The Whole Man." In *Rabindranath Tagore. Birthday Centenary Celebrations; Proceedings of Conferences, Vol. II.* Ed. Santosh Chandra Sen Gupta, Santiniketan: Visva-Bharati, 1961.

——. *The Volcano: Some Comments on the Development of Rabindranath Tagore's Aesthetic Theories and Art Practice.* Baroda: Maharaja Sayaji Rao University, 1967.

Andhra Pradesh Centenary Committee. *Tagore Centenary Number,* 1961.

Aronson, Alex. *Rabindranth Through Western Eyes.* Allahabad: Kitabistan, 1943.

Aurobindo, Sri. *The Renaissance in India.* 3rd ed., Calcutta: Arya Publishing House, 1946.

Ayyub, Abu Sayyeed. *Tagore's Quest.* Calcutta: Papyrus, 1980.

Banerjee, Hiranmay. *Rabindranath Tagore.* New Delhi: Publications Division, Government of India, 1971.

Banerjee, Srikumar, "Rabindranath's Novels." In *Homage to Rabindranath Tagore.* Ed. B.M. Chaudhuri. Kharagpur: Indian Institute of Technology, 1961.

Bhaskar, R.P. "The Novels of Tagore". In *The Genius of Tagore: Tagore Centenary Volume, Part I,* ed. Mahendra Kulasreshta. Hoshiarpur: V.V.R. Institute, 1961.

Bhattacharya, Bhabani. "Tagore as a Novelist" In *Rabindranath Tagore 1861–1961. A Centenary Volume.* Ed. S. Radhakrishnan. New Delhi: Sahitya Akademi, 1961.

Bhattacharjee, M.M. *Rabindranath Tagore: Poet and Thinker.* Allahabad: Kitab Mahal, 1961.

Bhattacharya, S. *Tagore and the World.* Calcutta: Das Gupta & Co., 1961.

Bhattacharya, Vivek. *Relevance of Tagore.* New Delhi: Metropolitan Book Co., Pvt. Ltd., 1979.

Bose, Budhadeva. *An Acre of Green Grass.* Calcutta: Orient Longmans, 1948.

Catlin, G.E.G., *Rabindranath Tagore.* Bombay: Allied Publishers, 1964.

Chakravorty, Amiya. *A Tagore Reader.* New York: The Macmillan Company, 1961.

Chakravorty, B.C. *Rabindranath Tagore: His Mind and Art.* New Delhi: Young India Publications, 1971.

Chandrasekharan, K. *Tagore, A Master Spirit.* Masulipatnam: Triveni Publishers, 1961.

Chattarji, Suniti Kumar. *Lectures on Rabindranath Tagore.* Aurangabad: Marathwada University, 1965.

Chaudhari, Prabas Jiban. *Tagore on Literature and Aesthetics.* Calcutta: Rabindra Bharati, 1965.

Chaudhuri, B.M. (ed.). *Homage to Rabindranath Tagore.* Kharagpur: Indian Institute of Technology, 1961.

Clark, T.W. (Ed.). *The Novel in India. Its Birth and Development.* London: George Allen and Unwin Ltd., 1970.

Cuthbertson, Carol. *Tagore an Artist.* Calcutta: Vidya-Bharati, 1968.

Dasgupta, Jayanta Kumar, "Some Recent Novels of Tagore," *Triveni,* Madras: March-April, 1935.

Das, Prafulla Chandra. *Tagore: The Poet of Light,* Cuttack-2, 1962.

Datta, K.K. *Socio-Cultural Background of Modern India.* Meerut: Meenakshi Prakashan, 1972.

Devi, Maitraye. *Tagore by Fire Side.* Calcutta: Rupa and Co., 1961.

Forster, E.M. "Two Books by Tagore." In *Abinger Harvest,* London: Edwin Arnold and Co., 1936; rpt. Pocket Edn., 1953.

Ghose, Sisirkumar. *The Later Poems of Tagore.* Bombay: Asia Publishing House, 1961.

——. *Rabindranath Tagore.* New Delhi: Sahitya Akademi, 1986, rpt., 1994.

——. *Tagore for You,* Calcutta: Visva-Bharati, 1965.

Ghosh, J.C. *Bengali Literature.* London: Oxford University Press, 1948.

Gokak, V.K. (ed.). *Literatures in Modern Indian Languages.* New Delhi: The Publications Division, Government of India, 1957.

Gopal, K. *Social Thought of Rabindranath Tagore.* Meerut: Arun Prakasan, 1974.

Gordon, Leonard A. *Bengal: The Nationalist Movement 1876-1940.* Delhi: Manohar Book Service, 1974.

Gowda, Annaiah. *Anjali: The Tagore Lectures.* Annamalainagar : Annamalai University, 1976.

Gupta, Nagendranath. *Seven Noble Lives.* (n.p.) 1950.

Gupta, Rameshwar. *The Essential Tagore.* (n.p.) 1961.

Hay, Stephen, N. *Asian Ideas of East and West, Tagore and His Critics in Japan, China and India.* Cambridge, Massachusetts : Harvard University Press, 1970.

Herman, H.L. "Gora as Traditional Literature," *The Visva-Bharati Quarterly,* Vol. 33, Nos. 384, 1967-68.

Iyengar, K.R. Srinivasa. *Indian Writing in English,* New Delhi: Sterling Publishers Pvt. Limited, 1984.

——. *Indo-Anglian Literature.* Bombay: Asia Publishing House, 1962.

——. *Rabindranath Tagore.* Bombay: Popular Prakashan, 1965.

——. "A General Survey," In *The Novel in Modern India,* ed. Iqbal Baktiyar. Bombay: The P.E.N. All India Centre, 1964.

——. *Rabindranath Tagore: A Critical Introduction.* New Delhi: Sterling Publishers Pvt. Ltd., 1987.

Iyengar, Masti Venkatesa. *Rabindranath Tagore.* Bangalore : Satyashodhana Pustaka Bhandara, 1946.

Kabir, Humayun. *Rabindranath Tagore: Tagore Lectures,* 1961. London: School of Oriental and African Studies, University of London, 1961.

——. *The Bengali Novel.* Calcutta: Firma K.L. Mukhopadhyay, 1968.

Khanolkar, G.D. *The Lute and the Plough, A Life of Rabindranath Tagore.* Transl. by Thomas Gay. Bombay: Book Centre Pvt. Ltd., 1963.

Kripalani, Krishna. *Rabindranath Tagore: A Biography.* London: Oxford University Press, 1962.

——. *Faith and Frivolity.* (n.p.) 1962.

——. *Tagore: A Life.* 2nd ed. New Delhi: Orient Longmans Ltd., 1971.

——. *Modern Indian Literature.* Bombay: Nirmala Sadanand, 1968.

Krishna Rao, A.V. *The Indo-Anglian Novel and the Changing Tradition.* Mysore: Rao and Raghavan, 1972.

Kulasreshta, Mahendra (ed.). *Tagore Centenary Volume.* Hoshiarpur: Visveshvaranand V.R. Institute, 1961.

Kumar, Anita S. "Tagore the Novelist: A Study of *Gora* and *The Wreck*," *Kakatiya Journal of English Studies,* 1 (March, 1975), 55-71.

Lal, P. *The Concept of an Indian Literature.* Calcutta: Writers Workshop, 1968.

Mani, R.S. *Educational Ideas and Ideals of Gandhi and Tagore.* (n.p.) 1961.

Mazumdar, Bimanbehari. *Heroines of Tagore.* Calcutta: Firma K.L. Mukhopadhyay, 1968.

Mazumdar, R.C. (ed.). "British Paramountcy and Indian Renaissance: Part II," *The History and Culture of Indian People,* Vol. X. Bombay: Bharatiya Vidya Bhavan, 1965.

——. "Struggle for Freedom," *The History and Culture of Indian People,* Vol. XI. Bombay: Bharatiya Vidya Bhavan, 1969.

Mehta, P.P. *Indo-Anglian Fiction: An Assessment.* Bareilly: Prakash Book Depot, 1979.

Mukherjee, Hiren. *Himself a True Poem: A Study of Rabindranath Tagore.* New Delhi: People's Publishing House, 1961.

Mukherjee, H.B. *Education for Fullness: A Study of the Educational Thought and Experiment of Rabindranath Tagore* (n.p.) 1962.

Mukherjee, Meenakshi. *Twice Born Fiction.* New Delhi: Arnold Heinemann, 1977.

Mukherjee, S.K. *Tagore for You.* Calcutta: Visva-Bharati (n.d.).

Mukherji, D.P. *Rabindranath Tagore* (n.p.), 1943.

Mukherji, S.B. *The Poetry of Tagore.* New Delhi: Vikas Publishing House, 1977.

Mukherji Dhurjati Prasad. *Tagore: A Study.* Calcutta: Manisha, 1972.

Mukherji, S., *Passage to America: The Reception of Rabindranath Tagore in the United States,* 1912-1941. Calcutta: Bookland Pvt. Ltd., 1964.

Mukherji, Probhat Kumar. *Life of Tagore.* Transl. by Sisirkumar Ghose. Delhi: Hind Pocket Books Pvt. Ltd., 1975.

Muley, D.S. *Ravindra Nath's Poetry.* Jabalpur: Universal Book Depot, 1964.

Neogy, Prithwish (ed.). *Rabindranath Tagore on Art & Aesthetics.* New Delhi: Orient Longmans Ltd., 1961.

Narasimhan, R. (ed). *Gurudev Tagore* (n.p. & n.d.).

Narain, V.A. *Social History of Modern India, Nineteenth Century.* Meerut: Meenakshi Prakashan, 1972.

Naravane, V.S. *An Introduction to Rabindranath Tagore.* Delhi: The Macmillan Company of India Ltd., 1977.

Padma, T. "Tagore's Binodini: A Re-appraisal." *Indian Scholar,* Raipur, July 1979.

Rabindranath Tagore in Perspective. Visva-Bharati, 1989.

Radhakrishnan, S. *The Philosophy of Rabindranath Tagore.* Baroda: Good Companions, 1961.

Raj, G.V. *Tagore: The Novelist.* New Delhi: Sterling Publishers, Pvt. Ltd., 1983.

Ray, Benoy Gopal. *The Philosophy of Rabindranath Tagore.* Bombay: Hind Kitabs, 1949.

Ray, Annadashankar and Lila. *Bengali Literature* (n.p.) 1942.

Ray, Lila. "The Novel," In *Bengali Language Handbook,* ed. Punyasloka Ray, *et al.* Washington: Centre for Applied Linguistics, 1966.

——. *A Challenging Decade* (n.p.) 1953.

Ray, Niharranjan. *An Artist in Life: A Commentary on the Life and Works of Rabindranath Tagore.* Trivandrum: University of Kerala, 1967.

——. "Three Novels of Tagore: *Chokher Bali, Gora, Yoga-Yoga,*" *Indian Literature,* IV (1961), 163-81.

Rhys, Ernest. *Rabindranath Tagore: A Biographical Study*. London: Macmillan & Co. Ltd., 1925.

Roy, Dilip Kumar. *Among the Greats*. Bombay: Jaico Publishing House, 1950.

Sahitya Akademi. *Indian Literature: Tagore Number*. New Delhi: 1961.

Sarkar, Samit. *The Swadeshi Movement in Bengal*. New Delhi: People's Publishing House, 1973.

Sastri, K.S. Ramaswami. *Rabindranath Tagore* (n.p.) 1916.

Sastry, C.N. *Walt-Whitman and Rabindranath Tagore: A Study in Comparison*. Delhi: B.R. Publishing Corporation, 1992.

Sen, Priyaranjan. *Western Influence in Bengali Literature*. 2nd ed. Calcutta: Saraswaty Library, 1947.

Sen, Sukumar. *History of Bengali Literature*. New Delhi: Sahitya Akademi, 1960.

Sen Gupta, Subodchandra. *The Great Sentinel: A Study of Rabindranath Tagore*. Calcutta: A. Mukherjee, 1948.

——. *Rabindranath Tagore: Homage from Visva Bharati*. Santiniketan: Visva Bharati, 1962.

Seth, Hira Lal. "Tagore's Novels," In *Tagore Centenary Souvenir*. Ed. Prakash Dewan Ram. New Delhi: Tagore Memorial Publications, 1961.

Sharma, K.K. *Rabindranath Tagore's Aesthetics*. New Delhi: Abhinav Publications, 1989.

Shriwadkar, Meena. *Image of Women in the Indo-Aglian Novel*. New Delhi: Sterling Publishers, 1979.

Singh, Baldev. *Tagore and the Romantic Ideology*. Calcutta: Orient Longmans, 1963.

Sinha, Sasadhar. *Social Thinking of Rabindranath Tagore*. Bombay: Asia Publishing House, 1961.

Srivastava, A.K., *God and Its Relation with the Finite Self in Tagore's Philosophy*. New Delhi: Oriental Publishers & Distributors, 1976.

Sykes, Marjorie. *Rabindranath Tagore* (n.p.) 1943.

Tagore and Man, Calcutta: Tagore Centenary Peace Festival All India Committee, November 1961.

Tagore, Rabindranath and Elmhirst, L.K. *Tagore, Pioneer in Education* (n.p.) 1961.

A Tagore Testament. London: Meridian Books, 1953.

Tagore, Rathindranth. *On the Edges of Time*. Bombay: Orient Longmans, 1948.

Tagore, Satyendranath and Indira Devi (tr. by). *The Autobiography of Maharshi Debendranath Tagore* (n.p.) 1916.

Tengshe, L.H. *Tagore and His View of Art* (n.p.) 1962.

Thompson, Edward. *Rabindranath Tagore: His Life and Work*. Rev. by Kalidas Nag. Calcutta: Y.M.C.A. Publishing House, 1961.

——. *Rabindranath Tagore: Poet and Dramatist*. London: Oxford University Press, 1926. Revised 1948.

Verma, Rajendra. *Men and Society in Tagore and Eliot* (n.p.) 1982.

Visva-Bharati Quarterly, The.

The Golden Book of Tagore: A Homage to Rabindra Nath Tagore. Ed. Ramananda Chatterji. Calcutta: Golden Book Committee, 1931.

Williams, H.M. *Indo-Anglian Literature 1800-1970: A Survey*. Madras: Orient Longman Ltd., 1976.

Books on Humanism

Baker, Herschell. *The Image of Man*. New York: Harper, 1961.

Blackham, H.J. *Objections to Humanism*. London: Constable & Co., Ltd., 1963.

Bush, Douglas. *The Renaissance and English Humanism*. Canada: University of Toronto Press, 1939; rpt. 1968.

Chakravarti, A. *Humanism and Indian Thought*. Madras: G.S. Press, 1937.

Chari, C.T.K. *Essays in Philosophy*. Madras: Ganesh & Co., Pvt. Ltd., 1962.

Chan, Wing-tsit (Tr. & Compiled). *A Source Book in Chinese Philosophy*. New Jersy: Princeton University Press, 1963.

Devaraja, N.K. *The Philosophy of Culture*. Allahabad: Kitab Mahal, 1963.

Fuller, B.A.G. *A History of Philosophy*, Part II. New York: Holt, Rinehart and Winston, 1964.

Huxley, Julian. *Essays of a Humanist*. London: Chatto & Windus, 1964.

——. *The Humanist Frame*. London: George Allen and Unwin, 1961.

——. *Man in the Modern World* (n.p. & n.d.).

——. *New Bottles for New Wine*. London: Chatto & Windus, 1957.

Jaspess, Karl. *Existentialism and Humanism*. New York: Russell F. Moore Company, Inc., 1952.

Kazin, Alfred. *On Native Grounds*. New York: Reynoal and Hitchcock, 1942.

Lamont, Corliss. *Humanism as a Philosophy*. New York: Philosophical Library, 1950.

Lin, Yutung (Ed. & Tr.). *The Wisdom of Confucius*. Random House, Inc., 1943.

——. *The Philosophy of Humanism*. London: Flek Books, 1958.

Mout, Kit. *What Humanism is About*. London: Barrie & Reckliff in association with Pemberton Publishing Co., Ltd., 1963.

Naravane, V.S. *Modern Indian Thought*. Bombay: Asia, 1964.

Radhakrishnan, S. *Eastern Religions and Western Thought*. London: Oxford University Press, 1940.

Radhakrishnan, S. and Raju, P.T. (ed.). *The Concept of Man*. London: George Allen and Unwin Ltd., 1960.

Rotenstreich, Nathan. *Humanism in Contemporary Era*. The Hague: Mouton & Co., 1963.

Sartre, Jean-paul. *Existentialism and Humanism*. London: Methuen, 1963.

Stace, W.T. *A Critical History of Greek Philosophy*. London: Macmillan Co., Ltd., 1962.

Teylor, Henry Osborn. *The Humanism of Italy*. New York: Collier Books, 1962.

Books on Nationalism, Indian Nationalism and Allied Topics

Banerjea, Surendranath. *A Nation in Making*. Madras: Oxford University Press, 1925.

Bora, Mahendra. *1857 in Assam*. Gauhati: Lawyer's Book Stall, 1957.

Bose, Nemai Sadhan. *The Indian National Movement*. Calcutta: Firma K.L. Mukhopadhyay, 1965.

Buckland, C.E. *Dictionary of Indian Biography*. London: Swan Sonnenschein, 1906.

Collet, Sophia Dobson. *The Life and Letters of Rammohun Roy*, ed. Dilip Kr. Biswas & Prabhat Ch. Ganguly. Calcutta: Sadharan Brahmo Samaj, 1965.

Das, Durga. *India from Curzon to Nehru and After*. London: Collins, 1969.

Dutt, K.N. *Landmarks in the Freedom Struggle of Assam*. Gauhati: Lawyer's Book Stall, 1958 (1969 edn.).

Emerson, Rupert. *From Empire to Nation*. Massachusetts: Harvard University Press, 1960.

Gokak, V.K. *English in India: Its Present and Future*. Bombay: Asia Publishing House, 1962 (1965 edn.).

Kohn, Hans *Nationalism: Its Meaning and History*. New York: D. Van Nostrand Co., 1955 (1965 revised edn.).

Macaulay, T.B. *Critical and Historical Essays*, 2 vols. London: J.M. Dent & Sons, 1963.

Majumdar, R.C. *History of the Freedom Movement in India.* 3 Vols. Calcutta: Firma, K.L. Mukhopadhyay, 1963.

Majumdar, R.C. Raychaudhuri, H.C. Datta, Kalikinkar. *An Advanced History of India.* London: Macmillan, 1963.

Minogue, K.R. *Nationalism.* London: B.T. Batsford Ltd., 1967 (London: Methuen, 1969).

Nayar, Kuldip. *India: The Critical Years.* Delhi: Vikas Publishing House, 1973.

——. *India After Nehru.* Delhi: Vikas Publishing House, 1975.

Prasad, Bisheshwar. *Changing Modes of Indian National.* New Delhi: People's Publishing House, 1966.

Rai, Lajpat. *Young India, 1916.* Delhi: Publication Division, 1968 edn.

Seal, Anil. *The Emergence of Indian Nationalism.* Cambridge: Cambridge University Press, 1968.

Smith, Vincent A. *The Oxford History of India.* Oxford: Clarendon Press, 1958 (3rd edn., ed. Percival Spear, 1964 reprint).

Tagore, Rabindranath. *Nationalism.* London: Macmillan, 1917; rpt. 1976.

Wedderburn, W. *Allan Octavian Hume.* London: C.B., 1913.

Other Books

Abrams, M.H. *The Mirror and the Lamp.* Oxford: 1953.

Allot, Miriam. *Novelists on the Novel.* London: Routledge and Kegan Paul Ltd., 1959.

Aristotle. *Aristotle's Theory of Poetry and Fine Art.* Transl. S.H. Butcher. Ludhiana: Kalyani Publishers, Indian Edition, 1974.

Benoit, Hubert. *Many Faces of Love.* London: 1955.

Block, Maxine (ed.). *Current Biography.* New York: The H.W. Wilson Company, 1942.

Cornford, F.M. *The Republic of Plato.* Oxford: 1941.

Edman, Irwin. *The World of Plato.* New York: 1927.

Freud, S. *New Introductory Lectures on Psycho-analysis.* London: 1957.

Henderson, Philip. *The Novel To-day.* London: Jane Lane, The Bodley Head, 1936.

Jones, Ernest. *The Life and Work of Sigmund Freud.* Penguin Books: 1957.

Jastro, Joseph. *Freud: His Dream and Sex Theories.* U.S.A.: Chilton Book Company, 1960.

Jung, C.J. *Psychological Types.* London: 1949.

——. *Symbols of Transformation.* New York: 1962.

——. *Collected Works of C.J. Jung.* London: 1959.

Knight, G. Wilson. *The Wheel of Fire.* London: Methuen & Co., 1949.

Lewis, F.R. *The Common Pursuit.* London: 1952.

Mordell, Albert. *The Erotic Motive in Literature.* New York: Collier Books, 1962.

Morgan, Douglas N. *Love, Plato, The Bible and Freud.* Bombay: Jaico Publishing House, 1966.

Narasimhaiah, C.D. *The Swan and the Eagle.* Simla: Indian Institute of Advanced Study, 1969.

Plato. *The Symposium.* Penguin Books: 1951.

Prabhavananda, Swami. *The Spiritual Heritage of India.* London: George Allen and Unwin Ltd., 1962.

Redpath, Theodore. *Tolstoy.* London: Bowes & Bowes, 1960.

Spencer, Dorothy M. *Indian Fiction in English.* Philadelphia: University of Pennsylvania Press, 1960.

Welleck, Rene and Warren, Austin. *Theory of Literature.* Penguin Books: 1973.

Index